PRAISE FOR
TODAY'S INNOVATOR

"This book is full of wisdom and stories related to the challenges facing Today's Innovators. Aaron Proietti is blunt about the harsh conditions that innovators encounter inside of organizations, and has now developed the playbook for facing them head on. This is a must read for anyone who must innovate."

— Maria Ferrante-Schepis, President, Maddock Douglas Inc.

"I have witnessed firsthand how Aaron Proietti uses the lessons inside of Today's Innovator to successfully create an environment where innovation thrives. Aaron will show you how to grow as an individual and leader, how to overcome barriers, and how to take measured risks to move your organization forward. Consider this book as your ultimate user's guide to innovation."

— Ed Walker, CEO, ArmadaGlobal

"I was lucky enough to learn from Aaron as a corporate leader. Now, he has become my personal mentor, and set me on a different career path than I ever thought possible. Getting insight from Today's Innovator into how he has done these things is literally the next best thing than doing it with him. It will propel your career."

— Mandy Webber, Director of Innovation, NewBoCo

TODAY'S INNOVATOR

How to Create an Environment Where Innovation Thrives

Shaun -
Go, Innovate!.

By Aaron Proietti

MOtivational PRESS®
LEADERS IN GLOBAL PUBLISHING

Published by Motivational Press, Inc.
1777 Aurora Road
Melbourne, Florida, 32935
www.MotivationalPress.com

Manufactured in the United States of America.

ISBN: 978-1-62865-593-3

CONTENTS

To Karen Proietti,
my tolerant wife,
and to my daughters,
Elizabeth and Sarah

ACKNOWLEDGEMENTS

Today's Innovator is the culmination of seventeen years of learning, failing, re-learning, and occasionally thriving, while innovating inside of complex organizations. It is based almost entirely on my experience, but has most certainly been shaped by dozens of innovators who are far more talented than I. I have observed, debated, and incorporated the best practices of these mentors, who have assumed many forms, from dynamic leaders to curious interns. Without their willingness to share with me their knowledge and experiences, this book would not have been possible. To everyone I've worked with who has shaped me and my career as an innovator, *thank you!*

While most of this book I contemplated and assembled alone, organizing patterns from the far reaches of my mind on my whiteboard, I'd specifically like to thank my friend Mandy Webber for her contributions throughout the process. Mandy questioned my approach to *Today's Innovator* at every turn, making many meaningful edits. She has always challenged me to be empathetic, and coached me to be bold.

It would be impossible to list all of my mentors along the way, but I know this book would not have taken this form without the influences of the following people in shaping my beliefs and challenging me to grow: Jory Berson, Tina DeSalvo, Jerry Elliott, Mark Dunlap, Chris Flint, Scott Ham, Lori Lovens, Laura Scully, Mrs. Steiper, and Ed Walker.

I would like to offer a big thank you to the many teams and teammates with whom I have experienced the innovation world: the YMCA Camp Cory staff of the 1990s; the PAY team at Capital One; the Project X team at Capital One featuring the innovators from Kuczmarski and Associates; the Capital One Small Business Credit Policy team; and the talented group at Heritage Union. From my time at Transamerica, I'd like to thank the ADMS Growth Initiatives team; the Transamerica Copernicus, Polaris and Orion teams featuring the expert innovators at Maddock Douglas; the Transamerica Executive Innovation Team, Extended Innovation Center Team, and Innovation Ambassadors; and the Transamerica Insights & Innovation Department and its leadership team. A special thank you goes to the Transamerica Life & Protection Innovation Center Team of Terry Matheny, Debbie Schwartz, David Eisenberg, Stephanie Tran, Trish Wethman, Mandy Webber, Bob Stellato, and Fallon Murray, for giving it a go with me and offering up blunt feedback every time it was needed.

Finally, thank you to my wife and family, as well as my parents, who throughout the years have supported me as I learned, traveled, job-hopped, worked strange hours, and decompressed from the constant battle to upset the status quo.

CHAPTER 1: YOUR INNOVATION COACHING GUIDE

Innovation initiatives inside complex organizations frequently, or nearly *inevitably*, fail to gain traction when they neglect to build and nurture innovation as a competency. Leaders grow impatient as their assigned innovators struggle to overcome the roadblocks they encounter. The result? Teams and innovators become stressed, conflicted, and confused as they fail to produce what's expected of them.

If this pattern sounds familiar to you or your organization, rest assured that you're not alone. As a former innovation leader myself, I have first-hand experience with the challenges that innovators face inside of complex organizations. *Today's Innovator* is a coaching guide for anyone who is expected to make high-impact decisions around innovation. I've developed the content in *Today's Innovator* to:

» Develop innovators who can plan and design a successful *innovation program* within complex organizations.

» Develop innovators who can facilitate the *mindset shift* required to ignite their innovation program.

» Transform individuals into *innovation leaders* who can create high-performing teams and environments to deliver on what's required of them.

» Propel organizations to higher levels of *innovation maturity.*

I have written *Today's Innovator* to coach you, as Today's Innovator, by combining my personal experiences with best practices that I've encountered throughout my career. My goal for this book is to simplify the approach to innovation for you and your organization, while appreciating and respecting the inherent complexity of innovation. But, this comes with the warning that no matter how much you simplify the approach, *innovation is not easy*. While some business decisions are linear (you choose to do x so that y happens), innovation doesn't often work that way. Innovation involves experimenting, adapting, and learning to continuously improve. Innovation is complex and nonlinear. You cannot predict with certainty how your innovation efforts will fare. The best you can do is improve your odds of success along the way. Further, the conditions need to be just right for innovation to take hold. Organizational leadership must support innovation; teams and employees must feel empowered.

KEY THEMES

It's important for you, as Today's Innovator, to understand the resisting, driving, and sustaining forces you are likely to encounter as you set out to innovate. Among these forces are many of the recurring themes that appear throughout the book. In the sections that follow, we'll explore each of these, and many others, in great detail.

The World is Changing. Fast. And there is nothing you, or your organization, can do to slow the pace of change. As we'll learn in the *Innovation Primer* that follows, this principle is the central tenet that innovators must internalize to understand both what innovation is, and why it's required.

Innovate...or Die. As the world inevitably passes us by, every organization will likely, at some point, turn to innovation as the remedy for getting ahead of, or at least keeping pace with, change. The reason for this is that business models and technologies tend to degrade in performance, or grow stale, over time. Restated: there is a limit to what a given business model or technology can contribute before experiencing diminishing returns. At that point, CEOs, executive teams, and leaders are forced to make a choice: innovate, or die. On the surface, the choice may seem obvious, but death may, in fact, be less painful than trying to get an entrenched organization or team to embrace innovation.

The Enemy of Innovation is the Status Quo. The reason innovation can be so painful is that it has a powerful enemy lurking around every corner and in every bush: the status quo. Every organization has an inertia producing repeatable, predictable results from an established way of doing things. This inertia, or gravity, is quite effective at keeping any disruptive influences or pressures at bay; and the gravity of the status quo is strong. Organizations that attempt to make superficial changes to become more innovative will find they'll tend to revert to old behaviors when the initial buzz of innovation wears off. Too many make the mistake of believing that a simple "declaration of innovation" will be sufficient to produce the desired result, but the status quo will never make innovation easy.

Innovation is Hard. Despite what some innovation books might claim, there is no perfect system of innovation that produces guaranteed results. Because of the complexity of the environment in which we are trying to innovate, there are no actions that can be prescribed which will produce innovative outcomes with any certainty. The best you can do is to improve your odds of success from innovation, by building and nurturing it as a competency. I used to tell my teams, "Innovation is not all Rubik's Cubes and Skittles," meaning they shouldn't expect that by setting up a room with easels and round tables, and spreading toys and candy on the tables, that innovation will occur. Today's Innovator must fight for every inch of progress, and will experience just as many setbacks as successes. To innovate, a special skill set that balances learning and performance is required.

Empathy and Empowerment. While there are many traits, values, mindsets, and skills that benefit innovators, empathy and empowerment are two of the most critical. The empathetic innovator favors learning over knowing, favors questions over answers. Through appreciation and respect for the status quo, the empathetic innovator is curious how their actions will impact their environment. The empowered innovator performs within an environment where risk-taking is acceptable; where collaboration is the rule, rather than the exception; and where creativity flourishes. Unfortunately, many innovators lack empathy or wait until it's too late for someone to empower them. The lesson you, as Today's Innovator, must learn is that no one will do these things for you — there is no guaranteed innovation system that can be installed that doesn't require an intimate, empathetic understanding of the status quo to install, and there is no magic wand for empowerment.

Demystify Innovation. Even with the right skill set, you will not succeed without a solid understanding of what is expected of you as an innovator. People have varying notions of what innovation is. Some think of it as product development, others as process improvement. Some think it is invention, others think it is ideation. When different stakeholders within an organization expect innovation to produce different results, it becomes a problem for the innovator; and far too often, this is the case. In order to set the conditions for success, leaders and innovators must make every effort to demystify innovation for the organization — to get every employee, every innovator, on the exact same page as to what is expected of them. The definition of innovation, for a given organization, at a specific point in time, must be relatable and accessible to those who are expected to innovate. You, as Today's Innovator, must understand both the reason for the innovation imperative, as well as the role you must play.

Mindset Shift to Innovation Leadership. Even if the notion of innovation is fully demystified for an organization's innovators, you will most likely not succeed if you approach innovation the way you approach, say, a technical or operational role in the same organization. Innovation is rarely successful if teams have rigid structures and if employees wait for direction that may never come. Organizations, teams, and individuals, must each make a mindset shift to *innovation leadership*. You must be willing to abandon traditional command-and-control structures to create the environment where innovation can thrive. Unfortunately, change is not easy. Everyone wants change, but they don't necessarily want to change themselves. Changing the mindset of an organization, team, or even yourself, requires a corresponding shift in strategy and culture to support and sustain innovation.

Innovation as a Competency, Not an Outcome. Perhaps the biggest mistake an organization or leader can make is to treat innovation as an outcome to be achieved. For the reasons I've begun to describe here, innovation efforts rub against the grain of an organization; you will meet heavy resistance and encounter seemingly insurmountable roadblocks at nearly every turn. Instead, innovation must be treated as a competency to be developed and nurtured. Innovation is not a switch that can be turned on, or a destination to be reached. It is best approached and built as a core competency that is essential to an organization's strategy and culture. However, as Today's Innovator, you can't expect that the conditions for innovation to occur will be built for you by some leader, committee, or consultant — you must develop yourself to be the agent of change. This book will arm you with information and perspective to allow you to transform yourself, and your organization, for innovation success.

BOOK OVERVIEW

The lessons in *Today's Innovator* are designed to benefit those who are designated innovation leaders — such as innovation department heads, Chief Innovation Officers, Chief Strategy Officers — but also to benefit *anyone who must innovate*, regardless of title. As long as you are expected to, or have a desire to, build a strong innovation competency within your organization, department or team, these lessons should apply. You need not be the Head of Innovation. Accountants, engineers, marketing leaders, and more, will all benefit from developing an innovation competency. This is Today's Innovator.

This book includes coaching on how Today's Innovator can develop innovation into a mature organizational competency, even if your organization today is wildly dysfunctional. Most importantly, this book is meant to inspire personal development — to set you up for success as an innovator and innovation leader. As a trusted colleague of mine once put it, "Make sure that you fix yourself before you attempt to fix others!"

Important Disclaimer: If you are looking for instruction on how to innovate — that is, if you're looking for an innovation process that guarantees success every time — then this book is not for you. For I assert that there is no process, organizational structure, office layout, reward structure, etc. for innovation that will guarantee results. The lessons in *Today's Innovator* are designed to shift your mindset so you can build and sustain an empowering innovation environment.

Here's how the book is organized:

CHAPTERS 1-4

In these opening chapters, you'll be introduced to the core themes and critical questions that recur throughout *Today's Innovator*. It is here where I'll introduce you to the *four stages of innovation maturity*. Then, we'll spend some time *demystifying innovation* — to take *innovation* from a commonly misunderstood notion to a term that is relatable and accessible to anyone expected to innovate. Finally, we'll begin to orient you, as Today's Innovator, to the role you will have to play in order to develop your organization's innovation competency.

PART 1: THE INNOVATION STRATEGY

In *The Innovation Strategy*, you'll learn how to assess the current trajectory of your organization, to uncover whether it is truly on track to meet its objectives. You will then learn how to inspire a shared vision of a future state, in which innovation is essential to the organization's strategy. You'll learn how to design an innovation strategy and how to build a roadmap to execute on bringing your organization from its current state, to its future state. We'll share examples of how various organizations set their vision. Then, we'll examine how innovation strategies may look in each of the four stages of innovation maturity. Finally, we'll share lessons to overcoming common modes of *resistance* or *roadblocks* that organizations encounter when trying to set innovation strategy.

PART 2: CULTURE OF INNOVATION

In *Culture of Innovation*, you will learn how your organization's culture impacts its ability to innovate. We'll explore what culture is, how it shows up, how it is reinforced, and how it might affect the outcomes you produce. You'll learn how to design culture that reinforces and sustains innovation. This will include an examination of your organization's values — both the values that are stated and reinforced today, as well as the values that your organization aspires to. We'll share examples of the stated values of various organizations. Similar to Part 1, we'll explore the quality of innovation-friendly values and culture in each of the four stages of innovation maturity. And, we'll again share lessons to overcoming cultural resistance and roadblocks.

PART 3: SYSTEMS OF INNOVATION

In *Systems of Innovation*, you'll learn how to identify and implement the *innovation governance systems* and *innovation ecosystems* that are right for your team or organization. When well-designed, *innovation governance systems* will dictate the rules and processes by which high-impact innovation decisions will be made. Your *innovation ecosystem* should be designed and iteratively improved to increase the effectiveness of innovation. We'll consider budgets, metrics, methods, processes, physical structures, reporting mechanisms, organizational schemes, and more. And again, we'll explore how these systems might appear in organizations in the four stages of innovation maturity, and address the resistance and roadblocks you may encounter.

PART 4: A PORTRAIT OF TODAY'S INNOVATOR

In this final part, *A Portrait of Today's Innovator,* we'll explore what is required of you as an *innovation leader* whose effectiveness relies on your ability to shift the organization's overall competency for dealing with change and complexity. Then, we'll explore what is required of an *individual* who is on the hook for building and launching innovations to improve an organization's capabilities and results. We'll cover a wide range of traits, from softer skills such as empathy, adaptability, influence, and motivation, to the technical skills most typically associated with innovators. I'll introduce you to the personas that you must embody as Today's Innovator, in order to truly feel empowered, to thrive in uncertainty, and to influence and motivate your teams and organizations to innovate.

CHAPTER 2: CREATING AN ENVIRONMENT WHERE INNOVATION THRIVES

For many organizations, their status quo is their competitive advantage, giving them reason to maintain their inertia, eliminate uncertainties, and to ward off threats. But the fate for most is stagnation and erosion in the form of performance degradation and/or lagging financials. This is particularly true in today's environment where the pace of change in the world is frenetic and accelerating. The organization's status quo will ultimately become an anchor, which makes growth and innovation challenging.

Today's business leaders face tremendous pressures to manage both short-term targets, as well as maintain a long-term vision for their organizations. Unfortunately, short-termism often trumps long-term decision-making. By the nature of the role, the CEO faces short-term pressures while simultaneously being asked about the future of the organization. The declaration that an organization will launch an innovation initiative is a common knee-jerk reaction to these pressures. Innovation, in this case, is viewed as a magic remedy to get the results where they need to be.

To many, innovation is sexy and buzzworthy because it means new and exciting things are coming. Nearly everyone wants it … until it requires YOU to change — your job, your title, your salary, your values, and your beliefs. Problems arise when innovation initiatives are launched inside of a system which must change to support them. When innovation doesn't "fit" into day-to-day operations, it is extremely difficult, if not impossible, to sustain it if the organization is not ready to change. Innovation initiatives that are bolted on to a stagnant business strategy face long odds of producing consistently favorable results. Such bolted-on efforts are unlikely to do much more than provide a short-term distraction from the erosion of the status quo. Sure, some innovation can be achieved in the absence of strong strategic alignment and cultural support, but it will compete with the organization's core business in a way that is not sustainable.

But let there be no doubt: The future is here, and it is wild. Organizations must constantly be asking: Where is the world going? What's our role in it? How must we change what we do today? What new opportunities exist?

Even if the answers are known, the anchors of the status quo must be identified and lifted. By making appropriate time and resource investments, organizations can become more nimble, responsive, and adaptive to the change factors they encounter. They can become more creative in the face of uncertainty. They can build the strategic and cultural structures necessary for innovation initiatives to take flight.

Innovation is not, of itself, a destination to be reached. It's a competency and mindset that enables some new destination to be attainable — some destination that the organization was not previously on track to reach. For innovation to become a core competency — one that is essential to the strategy and culture — organizations must take a well-paced and measured approach to ready themselves for change, and to subsequently change. Before the organization can be expected to innovate effectively, it must be your goal to create an environment where innovation thrives.

REWIRING THE ORGANIZATION

Creating an environment where innovation thrives is, by definition, an effort to bring into existence some aspirational future state of the organization (or at the very least to iterate the current state into some transitional state). But, whose job is it to reimagine or design the future state (or next iteration) of an organization? If it's left to the highest paid decision-makers, in addition to lacking the time to take a measured approach, these executives often lack an intimate understanding of how things really get done in their organizations. Their directives or vision may fail to appreciate and meet the organization where it is today. A collective effort, from those in the boardroom to those in the farthest reaches of the organization, is required to move an organization from its current state to its aspirational future state.

If you're expected to innovate, you're liable to feel like you're wasting away waiting for a well-articulated vision to come down from above, and you'll likely be disappointed when it finally comes. Today's Innovator cannot afford to idly wait for direction that may never come, or for a vision that might be unattainable. If it's unclear to you where the organization is headed, or how you're going to get there, it is empowering to embrace that it may be up to you to start the conversation, or insert yourself into the room where the innovation strategy is being developed.

The effort to design an attainable future state of any organization is not one to be taken lightly. We'll explore the process in depth, breaking it down into shifts in both strategy and culture, as well as changes to the systems of innovation that can make an innovation mindset possible and unlock new possibilities for a stale or slumping organization.

The change process is simple, and repeatable, but without deliberation steps are often skipped. These steps will reoccur throughout the course/ book:

Step 1: Assess the status quo

Step 2: Imagine and design a future state

Step 3: Develop a plan to get there

Step 4: Execute

Step 5: Iterate to become better

It's important to reiterate that when building the innovation competency, it is not sufficient to simply make a declaration that "We will now innovate!" The organization must be prepared for a long journey of iteratively promoting itself to higher levels of innovation maturity, measuring its progress, and reflecting along the way.

THREE CRITICAL QUESTIONS

As a leader or innovator striving to create an innovation-friendly environment inside a complex organization, there are three critical questions you must ask, answer, and revisit with regularity. For the answers to these questions inevitably change and therefore, so should the actions of the leaders and innovators.

#1: *What does the organization require from innovation in order to achieve its vision?*

The reason why any organization makes the choice of innovation (over death!) is that, most likely, it's not achieving, or on track to achieve, some long-term business objective. Restated, if the status quo were working, innovation would not be needed. In many organizations, it's quite obvious the status quo isn't quite working according to plan. There is always something that can be built or improved upon, such as a new capability or better results, respectively. This is where innovation comes in. Today's Innovator must be able to answer the question: What is required of innovation? Or, more completely: What is required of innovation to move the organization from where it is, today, to where it's going? If you're an innovator who doesn't know the answer to this foundational, critical question, drop everything you're doing right now and go find out the answer, because chances are you're working on the wrong things! If you cannot answer this question, you cannot be sure that your initiatives will deliver what the organization expects, or more directly, what the organization *requires* from innovation. Also, it should go without saying, but if you are an innovator who *does* know the answer to the critical question, and you're not working on whatever the answer is, you must consider if you're working on the wrong things.

We'll explore the process for asking, and answering this question in greater detail in *Part 1: The Innovation Strategy.*

#2: *What does the organization require from my team to achieve its objectives?*

To the extent that the first critical question addresses *what* the organization is expecting from innovation, the second addresses the *how*. Exploring the answer to this question can be the source of unlocking incredible potential in your innovation teams. Teams can improve and do better every day, but that won't happen unless they ask this question of themselves with regularity, rather than accepting their own status quo. Perhaps you need access to a new technology, knowledge of a new processes, or an expert opinion. Or, maybe there are cultural traits, norms, or values that are holding you back. Or, maybe the team isn't organized correctly and therefore, isn't achieving its potential. It's up to the team, comprised of innovators, to rediscover the answer regularly. Detached executives will only notice new team requirements when they show up as big problems, gaps, or deficiencies — at which point the executive will likely address them hastily or in a disruptive manner.

In *Part 2: Culture of Innovation*, we'll explore in depth the idea of sustainably changing the culture of teams and organizations, rather than changing superficial aspects of the organization. While more difficult to implement, shifting cultural traits, such as working norms and values, is far more likely to have a sustainable impact than changes such as adding project work, or introducing new rewards & incentives Then, we'll revisit this question in *Part 4: A Portrait of Today's Innovator.*

#3: *Who does the organization need me to be?*

Too often, employees fall into the trap of doing the same things over and over, each and every day, because that's what they believe is expected of them. Or, employees do the things that someone, at some distant time, said they should be working on. Worse, many employees will *only* do what they have been told to do, and won't work on anything they haven't been asked to. Unfortunately, for that employee and the organization, that work may not be what the organization *truly needs*. It is only from your unique vantage point as an individual, and from your unrelenting passion to ask and answer this third critical question, that this pattern of helplessness can be broken, and you can begin to mature as an innovator. Maybe you need to be a better leader. Maybe you need to be more collaborative. Or, maybe you need to prioritize your work in order to achieve the results the organization truly needs to you to produce.

In *Part 4: A Portrait of Today's Innovator*, we will explore the traits, skills, and mindsets that are required of Today's Innovator, and these should be considered when answering this critical question of who the organization needs you to be.

CHAPTER 3: THE FOUR STAGES OF INNOVATION MATURITY

Many organizations taking their first steps towards developing an innovation competency will (falsely) believe that just by carving out some nominal resources (typically a few quasi-dedicated employees with a tiny budget), they could become the next big industry disruptor — the next Netflix or Uber. They are unaware (perhaps innocently) of the long odds, the innumerable obstacles, the unrealistic expectations that their innovation efforts will face. When these efforts fail to produce what's expected, the resources are redeployed and innovation is forgotten...until the next *innovate or die* crossroads is encountered.

Such organizations will remain stuck in a cycle of *dysfunctional innovation,* feeding a "flavor of the month" attitude towards organizational buzzwords. They will eventually face the realization that innovation is a competency to be developed and nurtured, rather than an outcome to be desired or purchased. Only once they enter into a well-considered change process can they truly promote their business to higher levels of innovation maturity, and thereby reasonably expect to achieve more consistent results.

Below are *four stages of innovation maturity* that organizations might expect to attain as they develop their innovation programs and competency. Organizations will hopefully advance amongst these stages, but despite their best efforts, may occasionally retreat as conditions change. Some setbacks are to be expected. What's important for your organization is to have a realistic understanding of both where you are at any point in time along this scale, and why your organization is at that stage, so that you may design an approach to continue to mature.

DYSFUNCTIONAL MATURITY STAGE

Most organizations will classify into this stage. The term "dysfunction" does not imply that an organization in this stage is "incapable," but that the odds of delivering on lofty innovation objectives are long. Many of these organizations will completely lack any defined innovation objectives, rendering nearly impossible the likelihood that the objectives are attained. Employees of organizations in this stage likely aren't in tune with the pressures the organization is facing, and therefore, don't have an understanding of why innovation might be required. The employees asked to innovate may not feel adequately supported, or may not have the skills to be successful, or both.

An example of a well-known company that seems to be stuck in this stage is United Airlines. Following multiple public relations disasters — from breaking guitars (look up "United Breaks Guitars"), to forcefully dragging out a bloodied passenger who committed the sin of possessing an oversold seat, to negligently killing a puppy by ordering a passenger to put it in an overhead bin — United has reiterated their commitment to changing, but the results don't follow. United's publicly stated values ("Fly the Friendly Skies") likely don't match their real organizational values, making meaningful change challenging. Their focus should be on setting off on a deliberate journey to attaining a more desirable future state, rather than on repeatedly making the empty declaration that they will do better.

TENTATIVE MATURITY STAGE

Organizations who fall in this maturity stage openly recognize that innovation is important to the strategy. Innovation has been introduced into the common language of the organization, but may be viewed by employees as "that thing that happens somewhere else," referring to some team or department that is far removed from them. These organizations may make some changes, such as creating a dedicated innovation team, but will fail to make many of the environmental changes (strategic, cultural, or systems-related) required for innovation to thrive. There may be a belief that great *ideas* will lead to breakthrough innovation, but many innovation initiatives will grind to a halt after the ideation stage. Employees may be excited by the notion of innovation, but the lack of an empowering environment will produce a timid response. Organizations may begin to feel conflicts in values arise, and will importantly start to question *why*, but will not have yet taken the steps towards inspiring meaningful, systemic change.

An example of a company that seems to be currently in this stage is the United States Postal Service. In 2016, the USPS publicly released a well-considered five-year strategic plan titled *Future Ready.* The plan paints a picture of the current environment of the USPS, which makes clear the case for innovation. However, the plan does not address the very real conflict that innovation, particularly in the case of automation, may further reduce the quantity of employees needed to operate. The plan goes so far as to state that employees must be "equipped, empowered, and engaged," to deal with customers effectively, but does not outwardly reconcile the fact that automating processes and digitizing customer experience will likely further distance employees from their customer.

CONFIDENT MATURITY STAGE

For organizations in this stage of maturity, innovation is consistently planned for, and becomes ancillary to the strategy. It is well understood that innovation is a priority. It has been woven into some governance structures and innovators are accountable for delivering projects, which the organization requires. Innovation activities may take place in skunkworks operations, or as separate departments in an attempt to keep innovation separate from the core operations. Grass roots initiatives that encourage employee ideation and co-creation may gain some traction. Some innovation success may have been met, but it may also have experienced a fast burn, and ultimately cannot be sustained. To executives with their heads in the clouds, it may appear as though the organization has transformed, but legacy narratives and systems continue to anchor the organization to its past. The "new" business competes with the "core" business for resources. The confidence of an organization in this maturity stage may be a false arrogance. They may revert back to Tentative Maturity when innovation doesn't deliver what's expected, to reconsider their approach.

An example of a company in this stage is a former employer of mine, Transamerica, an insurance, investment, and retirement company. After reworking its identity over a period of several years from a dozen or more separate companies to one of "One Transamerica," innovation teams and departments have become well-formed. The language of innovation is well-known. Employees expect to hear about innovation and expect to be invited to participate in innovation initiatives regularly. However, the core strategy of the business remains one of "operational excellence," which requires extensive cost-cutting, an acute focus on quality, and a rationalization in the customization of offerings to "fewer, done well." As a result, innovators trying to integrate their work back into the core business must compete for the same resources that are consolidating business systems and "keeping the lights on." At times, Transamerica might revert back to Tentative Maturity, or even advance forward to Competent Mastery, but its tendency is to quickly snap back into the Confident Maturity Stage.

COMPETENT MASTERY STAGE

For organizations in this maturity stage, innovation is essential to the strategy. There is likely no difference between the organization's "core" strategy and the innovation strategy. These organizations have learned to reward values, not outcomes, to ensure that the behaviors which drive innovation are sustained. Structures, such as organizational charts, HR competency models, hiring practices, and business processes sustain and self-reinforce innovation as an integral competency of the organization. Restated, innovation is everywhere. Innovation is no longer "that thing that happens somewhere else." In fact, the term *innovation* is redundant and may not even be used. Empowered employees lead the innovation charge. Organizations in this stage may run the risk of struggling to operationalize and scale their successful innovation initiatives.

A well-known example of a company in the Competent Mastery Stage is Tesla. From their vision of reimagining the way that cars are built (sustainably) and purchased (directly), to their investments in battery technology, driverless automation, solar technology, and much more, it is clear that innovation is essential to, and indistinguishable from, their business strategy. Employees embrace change and drive continuous improvement. Recent struggles to scale their Model 3 sedan production processes to meet demand, however, have exposed a wart, as Tesla doesn't yet have a proven track record of maintaining profitable, at-scale business.

CHAPTER 4: DEMYSTIFYING INNOVATION

Before going further, let's take some time to get on the same page regarding what is meant by *innovation*. It's funny (as well as a bit sad) to note that a full 80% of all speakers at innovation industry conferences will begin their presentations by citing the Merriam-Webster's Dictionary definition of "innovation." Of course, I made that statistic up for effect, but the point is this: *innovation* has been a mystical corporate buzzword for twenty-five years or more, and its mystique, shows no signs of abating. While I will spare you the true dictionary definition of the term, I will define it in a way that demystifies the term by replacing the buzzworthiness with a practical, broad applicability. Not to belabor the point, but imagine going to an accounting conference only to find that all the speakers felt it necessary to share the dictionary definition of *accounting* at the outset of every presentation. You'd have difficulty taking either the speaker, or the industry, seriously!

In 2012, I led a corporate initiative to transform a culture from a hierarchical culture of compliance, to a culture of innovation, collaboration, and trust. This notion of a "culture of innovation" carried with it all the buzz that you might expect inside of a traditional corporate organization. I had an opportunity to travel to our major North American offices and host large "Culture of Innovation Café" sessions, to orient each of our 6,000 employees to the new culture. After introducing myself from the large stage, I looked out over the crowd of employees and simply asked, "What is Innovation?"

Without hesitation, all of the canned replies came back at me. "It's ideation!" would be shouted from a front table. Someone would yell out, "Creativity!" from a table in the back. "Invention" would also be heard, as would "New Products" and "New Services." A more erudite employee would raise his hand waiting to be called upon, only to utter the predictable, "It's something new, which adds commercial value," or something similar. It struck me that *the only consistency in the replies was that innovation was inconsistently understood.* While the inconsistency did offer some flexibility as to how the term would ultimately be applied, the big risk was that the notion's ambiguity would never be resolved — and therefore never advance beyond the buzz.

This simple anecdote illustrates the point that successful innovation in a complex organization requires demystifying the term for employees. In the absence of a commonly understood definition, any innovation objective would be automatically unattainable since the objective would never be agreed upon. After all, if everyone thinks *innovation* means something different, can it even happen? For some, *innovation* is an aspirational notion; for others, it is almost clinical. In order for any innovation objective to be attained, the term *innovation* must be made both relatable and accessible for any employee expected to innovate.

Similar to how US Supreme Court Justice Potter famously said of *obscenity*, "I know it when I see it," it seems that *innovation* has a form that everyone recognizes, but that few are able to articulate. To reach an agreeable definition that will allow us to continue to explore *innovation* as a competency for the remainder of this book, let's first reach a common understanding of *why* and *when* innovation is needed (relying on the fact that we all at least have a notional understanding of the term.)

The first time an office worker might hear the term *innovation,* it might come from the mouth of a CEO or business leader describing how the business must elevate its performance to exceed even the most aggressive expectations. As I've previously alluded to, this is likely nothing but a thinly veiled admission that the business is not currently on track to achieve some objective that some power believes it should be achieving. This situation likely arises as a previously reliable product, technology, or business model begins to grow stale. Further investment in this product, technology, or business model would likely produce diminishing returns. The CEO or business leader is telling you that the status quo has begun to stop working.

If you're faced with this situation — that your organization is not on track to achieve its objectives — here's an exercise you can conduct: first, assemble your best thinkers in a room, describe the situation, and ask: "Why are we not achieving our objectives?" You're likely to get some surface-level observations, such as "Our strategy is not well defined," or "We're not executing fast enough," or "We don't take risks," or "We don't have the right people," or "Our competition delivers everything before we do," etc. Follow each of those statements with a second "Why?" and you'll begin to uncover some of the real issues facing the organization.

"Our strategy is not well defined."

"Why?"

"Because our leadership team can't agree upon a direction."

Then, continue to go deeper, "Why?"

"Well, they don't meet enough, and when they do, they report only on their current results with no talk about our strategy."

"Why?"

And so on. Now, let's do another one, to look for patterns.

"We're not executing fast enough."

"Why?"

"Because our best resources are over-extended."

"Why?"

"Because there are too many priorities."

"Why?"

And so on. This exercise is called, "Five Whys," as the utility tends to degrade by the fifth level. At the end of the exercise, you'll have a rich list of dysfunctions and seemingly insurmountable challenges that the organization currently faces. The way through may not be clear, but it will at least be obvious to the whole room that *something* needs to change. (Note: sometimes, the conversation will stop here because complex business problems are hard to deal with! This is where *innovation* might get introduced as the perfect remedy for all of these issues. But Today's Innovator must have the mettle to face the complexity head-on, in order to move past the buzzword remedy.) A close inspection of the potentially dozens of whys will likely show a pattern. Any of the whys could be classified into one of these four categories:

A. Our strategy is insufficient

B. Our culture is insufficient

C. We don't have the proper systems of innovation (e.g. rules, procedures, talent, and decision structures)

D. The world is changing around us

While there may be a few outliers, each of the whys will generally fall into category A, B, C, or D. At the conclusion of this exercise, it should be abundantly clear that innovation (whatever that is) is necessary. Further, you have now gained the added clarity that it's necessary *because* your strategy, culture, and systems of innovation are insufficient to keep pace with the world changing around you.

This brings us to our practical, broadly applicable definition of *innovation* that I promised:

Innovation is the core organizational competency for dealing with the everyday, aggressive pace of change.

But, wait, you're thinking. *That's not innovation! Innovation is supposed to be about ideas and invention. Innovation is supposed to be exciting and sexy! It's supposed to be sticky notes and offsite meetings. It's supposed to be Rubik's Cubes and a bowl of Skittles in the middle of a round table!*

For sure, this isn't your traditional, buzzworthy definition of innovation. But, it most certainly does not prohibit or preclude any of the short replies I heard blurted out from that stage. Whichever form it takes, if it helps the organization deal with change, innovation *can be* ideation, invention, a new product, or even the name of a department. It can be some, all, or none of those things. When viewed as an outcome, innovation is either successful or it is not. By positioning it as a competency, it offers hope that it can be trained and developed to improve the odds of success. It is the competency which helps the organization overcome perhaps its biggest stressor, namely, *change*.

THE ROLE OF TODAY'S INNOVATOR

As Today's Innovator you will struggle to succeed in your innovation efforts without a solid understanding of the challenges your organization faces. This understanding can be attained through thorough consideration of the *change factors* that face your organization. These change factors may be internal, such as poor quarterly earnings, the announcement of a new strategy, big projects tying up key resources, a reorganization, the acquisition of a new technology, or the launch of a new brand. Many will be external, such as changing consumer preferences, new product offerings from competitors, the emergence of new technology platforms, regulatory advances, or the appearance of potentially disruptive startups.

Once these change factors are well understood, you can begin to question whether you, or your team, or your organization, have the right traits and capabilities to identify new change factors and respond to those you're facing. For instance, do you have sufficient learning agility? Do you research consumer behaviors? Are you creative? Are you experimenting? Are you inspired? Is morale high? Do you have enough influence in the organization? Enough expertise? Are you collaborating effectively? Armed with the results of this survey of your traits and capabilities, you can then address any deficiencies by developing plans to become more responsive to change factors.

The definition of innovation as the core organizational competency for dealing with the everyday pace of change is a call to action: you must identify change factors, evaluate capabilities, develop response options, and then respond. Further, it is a call to action for you to conduct this exercise regularly, as the pace of change in the world today is accelerating. This effort to collect evidence of change and improve your capabilities and responsiveness will rarely be "assigned" to you by someone in charge. It's up to you to initiate and repeat these exercises to be best prepared for the changes you will face. It is your ability to readily identify changes and master the traits and capabilities required to respond that will ultimately determine your success as an innovator.

As Today's Innovator, you must be self-aware, multi-dimensional, continuously improving, curious, and empathetic, in order to become nimble, responsive, and adaptive in the face of change. You must be capable of using an appropriate mixture of front-end innovation methodologies, such as consumer research, ideation sessions, or hackathons, and back-end methodologies, such as Agile, Lean Startup, Stage-Gate processes, or prototyping. You must have the ability to engage support resources, as well as influence decision makers. You must be able to develop and display any number of other traits, as needed, in order to *be who the organization needs you to be.*

As Today's Innovator, you must become an *innovation leader* who ensures the conditions are right for innovation to occur, the strategy is aligned, the culture is supportive of innovation, and the innovators around you feel empowered to deliver on what the organization requires.

Innovation leaders are not born this way. They develop the muscle to learn fast, but to slow down when required. They ask critical questions, and truly listen to what others have to share. They experience the same pressures as others, but adapt and respond in a manner that impresses, if not inspires. The best leaders, in this respect, are not always the people-managers; they are the individuals who learn to lift others up with them as they grow. They are the individuals who learn the most about changes that the organization is experiencing. They are the individuals who create safe spaces for important dialog to occur.

These particular traits of an innovator will not show up on a job description. They're not taught in M.B.A. programs. And for many, like me, they don't come naturally.

When I first attained the title of Chief Innovation Officer, I believed it would be my role to build cool conference rooms with easels and beanbag chairs, and host ideation sessions throughout the company. However, a few months in, I began to learn that innovation success in a complex organization depended far less on my creativity and more on my ability to have empathy, to connect people with strategy, and to trust and learn alongside my team. I have two math degrees, and had used my quant skills to develop a strong proficiency in managing products and business processes. It turns out that these credentials were, at best, just a basic requirement to get the job. By no stretch of the imagination would they prove to be success factors for me in my innovation leadership role. To be an innovation leader, I had to relearn everything I thought I knew about innovation. The ideas, the creativity — even developing the concepts and prototypes — these were the easy parts. Learning how to create the conditions for success was the challenge. I wrestled with the challenge of understanding what our strategy required from innovation. It wasn't clear how our culture operated. I was unsure how to negotiate for shared resources, or how to integrate "new stuff" into the "core business." For me, there was no handbook. It is my hope that this book can serve as your guide, or at the very least your compass, as you navigate your way to becoming a Competent Master of innovation, and as you develop into *Today's Innovator*.

PART 1: THE INNOVATION STRATEGY

For an organization to set sail several ships in the direction of new, uncharted territory, that is brave! It is a sound strategy to test many routes, in order to improve the odds of reaching beyond the horizon. Many of those ships won't make it. For those that survive, the crews may look very different when they arrive. But, never be fooled into thinking any of those ships could ever reach the moon.

I will forever remember the date — June 2, 2015. A party orchestrated in five cities across the country: the Insights & Innovation department was turning two years old. A passionate, cross-functional team had designed and planned the party, and team leaders were hosting the party at each site. I, personally, had traveled to join the team in Los Angeles, and could feel the energy from the other sites when we dialed into the video conference.

This birthday party was more significant than simply a two-year anniversary celebration for a department. The department, itself, was the most visible and notable symbol of the investment that Transamerica was making in innovation. Amidst the turbulence of a whirlwind of organizational change all around us, the Insights & Innovation department had developed a new and exciting identity. As its leader, I had taken many risks to prove to the team members that this department was unique — that we would work differently than any of us had before. We emphasized collaboration and curiosity, risk-taking and continuous improvement. We had built a new culture that hadn't before existed at this company. And it was on this department's second birthday that we would unveil a new strategy, one that its leadership team had been designing for weeks: Insights & Innovation 2.0.

We had developed a new department logo for the party. All attendees got a coffee mug. Each site had their own celebratory offerings; I seem to recall there was candy and champagne in the Los Angeles office. It was no secret we were launching a new strategy, as transparency and co-creation had become primary cultural values of ours, but there was still a great deal of suspense.

In many respects, this celebration was the culmination of many years of my work as an innovation leader in a complex organization. It was no easy road to get to this place, and it wouldn't get any easier from here on out. Unbeknownst to the dozens of employees who, together, had so intimately experienced the struggle to get here, there was much more turbulence coming. At the same time we were designing this next-generation strategy for the Insights & Innovation department, I was called upon to work with those at the highest levels of the organization to, yet again, completely upend any of the organizational stability that we had attained. Within six months of this date, the Insights & Innovation 2.0 strategy would become irrelevant, as the company would announce a reorganization that would be far too substantial for Insights & Innovation to survive as a department in any recognizable form. Within one year, to the day, I would "retire" from corporate America on a quest to learn what I wanted to be when I grow up.

At this point, you may be wondering why a departmental birthday party with a presentation on a new strategy that would become obsolete within just a few months would persist as a remarkable memory for me. And the answer is simple; it was the best strategy work I had ever been part of. It had a compelling vision, it reframed our purpose as a department, and it facilitated a future-oriented mindset shift that I had been unsuccessful in prior attempts to inspire.

It was prophetic as well — prophetic of the changes to come. In doing the legwork to understand what change factors we faced, my leadership team had concluded that the world, as we knew it today, was going to change, and was going to change fast. While we didn't understand the precise form or timing of any particular changes, we had picked up on the signals, strong and weak. There were significant forces acting upon the teams, the department, divisions, country units, company, and industry. The economics of the business were stressed, the regulatory environment was volatile, consumer preferences were shifting, and more. In this aggressively changing business environment, there would be added pressures, such as new leadership demands, new talent demands, knowledge demands, technical demands, intense marketplace competition, new regulation, and more.

Now, these conditions aren't unique to Transamerica in 2015. They are being felt everywhere in varying forms and intensities. What was special about this particular point in time was that an entire department came together to develop a common understanding of what was required of us. Thorough planning in response to change factors had inspired a shared vision of what we could become.

Whether or not our vision was ever attained is debatable, as the coming organizational changes would strip Insights & Innovation of its identity. But the question seems unimportant. Strategy is iterative. Changing business and environmental conditions must necessarily and regularly change strategy. The Insights & Innovation 2.0 strategy was just an iteration — no more or less important than any iteration before, or that would follow — with one exception: that all of its elements had come together at the exact same time. Rarely in your career will you experience such a convergence of strategic planning work streams — it only happened once for me.

* * *

Many organizations declare innovation a priority, but few go far enough to describe just *how* innovation will contribute to achieving their goals. In the absence of this direction, innovators are virtually guaranteed to miss their mark, ultimately leaving innovation itself as a failed experiment. In *The Innovation Strategy,* we will explore how to develop and execute strategy, to set up Today's Innovators for success.

There are strong arguments on both sides of whether it is more important to first establish a supportive work culture or a sound innovation strategy when launching an innovation program. In the absence of a definitive answer to the question, we'll start with a deep exploration of *strategy*. It would be a challenge, to say the least, to attempt to redesign and change a culture without a clear understanding of what it is you, as Today's Innovator, are expected to accomplish.

To begin, we'll provide a *Strategy Primer*, in which we'll consider the general case of the steps an organization might take when developing its overall strategy, define the common terms you're likely to run into when building a strategy, and establish the *Role of Today's Innovator* in building an organization's strategy. Then, in *Innovation Strategy Development*, we'll get into the distinction between an organization's overall strategy and its *innovation strategy*. In *Roadmap, Execution, & Iteration*, you'll learn how to build an *innovation roadmap*, how to increase your odds of success in executing your innovation strategy, and some approaches to establishing a cadence for strategic iteration. We'll end with a review of the *Innovation Maturity Stages*, followed by discussion on how to overcome *Resistance and Roadblocks* that you may face as you develop your innovation strategy.

CHAPTER 5: A STRATEGY PRIMER

The stereotype of the corporate innovator is the creative genius, or the inventor, who, unencumbered by rules, mixes and matches features or ingredients, until he creates something that defines an entirely new product category. While this notion is romantic — that your organization will be saved by the ideas of some castaway employee tinkering in a dark corner — relying on this approach would be considered reckless. The truth is that innovation inside a complex organization can require strict discipline and direction. Without reason to believe that your innovation program will produce results, leaders will be quick to shut it down and redirect its resources. The development and socialization of a sound innovation strategy can give the organization a high degree of faith that its innovation investment is a smart one.

GENERAL STRATEGY DEVELOPMENT

To start our exploration of how to build a sound innovation strategy, let's first establish an understanding of how business strategy is developed. The steps that follow offer a formula for strategy development. Unfortunately, it is common for organizations to skip important steps, leading to an inability to execute on their strategy. The process is simple, yet the risk in skipping a step can be severe.

Step 1: Assess the Current State

Step 2: Articulate the Future State Vision

Step 3: Develop the Roadmap

Step 4: Execute the Plan

Step 5: Iterate

It's important to start with a *current state assessment* to understand A) the capabilities and resources of the organization, B) what the organization is on track to accomplish, and C) what challenges or changes the organization will face on its current track.

In the case of A, failure to take this step can result in a situation where the strategic demands exceed the current potential of the organization, such as in cases where it is incorrectly assumed that a certain technology competency is sufficiently well-developed. Nearly all organizations regularly conduct thorough forecasting and budgeting exercises to understand B. C can be assessed through an analysis of *change factors*, that is, what is changing, when it might change, and how changes might impact their organization.

For many organizations, change factors are blind spots. Unforeseen change factors are often the very catalyst for a CEO to declare that *innovation* will save the organization. This is not to say that CEOs are ill prepared to run their own businesses. Rather, it's a nod to the complexity of today's world in that previously unknown forces or entities can completely upend or disrupt a strategy in the blink of an eye. It's not reasonable to say that it is the CEO's role, alone, to prepare for these change factors. It is an essential role for you as Today's Innovator to play, to detect signals, strong and weak, from a wildly complex landscape, and to develop well-formed notions of potential changes in regulations, customer preferences, consumer trends, competitive launches, startups, etc.

Once the current state is understood, the organization must then attempt to get on the same page with respect to where the organization is headed, for great strategy is a product of a great *vision*. An organization's *vision* answers the question of "What does success look like?" It can also be thought of as an organization's *ambition*. It is often time-boxed, described as what an organization will achieve *x* years into the future. The most critical aspect of a sound vision statement is that it is developed as a collectively desired, or *shared*, vision. A shared vision is one to which each contributing member can feel a personal connection. This shared vision should be aspirational (a stretch), compelling (it matters to the team), and directional (it's clear which way to go). Failure to articulate an aspirational, compelling, directional, and time-bound vision can result in varying interpretations or misunderstandings of what the organization is trying to achieve.

In eleventh grade, I had the opportunity to travel to Paris with my high school French class. Despite five years of French classes, I still could not speak the language. There was one afternoon where we split up into small groups, and were expected to meet back at a particular place in the city at a particular time. However, when the time came, my group was stuck wandering the streets of Paris, not knowing how to pronounce, locate, or navigate to our intended destination. In hindsight, it would have been much easier if we had decided to meet up at the Eiffel Tower at the chosen time. Then, to locate our meeting place, we had to do nothing more than simply look up in the sky, then walk towards the tower.

If everyone knows that's where you are headed, they can all simply look up and head in that direction. The vision of the organization should be its Eiffel Tower. Once the work is done to create a clear and compelling future state vision, each department, team, and individual, including the innovators, will be inspired to develop their own approach to getting there. Executive leaders, instead of directing the activities of the entire organization, can spend their time surveying the landscape and communicating any additional change factors as threats or opportunities to those on the streets.

Below are some examples of vision statements from well-known companies. Some meet several of the criteria of being a strong vision statement, some do not. Explore for yourself:

» Tesla: To create the most compelling car company of the 21st century by driving the world's transition to electric vehicles.

» USPS: Postal services that customers value in a digital economy.

» American Express: Make American Express the world's most respected service brand.

» Google: To provide access to the world's information in one click.

» American Red Cross: The American Red Cross, through its strong network of volunteers, donors and partners, is always there in times of need.

There is no initial requirement to prove that the vision is possible to achieve. It is more important to be sure that the vision is what the organization wants to become, and that it is clear and unambiguous. Once an organization has articulated its vision it can then develop its *strategy* to answer the questions, "How will we achieve the vision?" or "What will it take?" It is just as important for a strategy to inform what should be done, as it is to inform what should not be done.

Strategies are built in context of the change factors and constraints of an organization as a set of actions, which will move it from its current state to some future state (its shared vision). An understanding of change factors allows the strategy to be focused to pursue specific *strategic vectors* or *strategic priorities*, which will position an organization for future success. This involves developing a strategic response to a change factor or a set of change factors.

At a previous employer of mine, in response to rising customer acquisition costs, we developed a "lifetime customer value" strategic vector, to develop a set of capabilities and deliver a set of outcomes, which would shift the business model away from being acquisition-focused. This new strategic vector placed greater emphasis on customer relationships and their lifetime value potential. Another example may be a strategic vector to identify and install technologies which would allow automation of high-cost or inconsistent operational process, such as a digitalization strategy.

However, it is not enough to simply focus the strategy by identifying change factors and strategic vectors. The ultimate test is for organizations to *execute* rapidly and *iterate* regularly to deliver on their strategy. Once the vectors are identified, the organization can begin to identify specific strategic *objectives* that should be met. These objectives might be capabilities to be developed, insights to be gained, or outcomes to be achieved, in order to make progress on the strategic vectors.

Consider the metaphor of a lost driver running out of gas on the way to an evening party. His original directions will no longer get him to where he's going — after all, he's lost. In this case, it's not his strategy to get to the party on time. That's his vision. Neither is it his strategy to hike to a gas station. That's an objective. Strategy is the art and science of making choices to move from the current situation to a better situation, closer to the vision. Our driver's strategy could then include the hike, finding money to pay for the gas, and devising a plan to return to the car with enough gas in hand to get to the party. Although, even that strategy would be a very basic strategy. It is also important for him to understand the pressures, or forces, that may act against him now, or that he may encounter down the line, such as solving for the fact that he is lost, making sure his appearance is proper once he arrives at the party, planning for bad weather on his hike, etc. In such a situation, he will no doubt continually survey the landscape, making quick decisions and maybe even changing strategy when he has enough data, or insight, to be reasonably certain of outcomes.

In order to address competing priorities and eliminate inefficiencies that might arise from lack of sufficient planning, the organization must develop a plan, or a *strategic roadmap*. A strategic roadmap clarifies strategic priorities, defines strategic vectors, and spells out the various objectives that have been identified. Further, the roadmap should identify the resources and lay out the framework that will be used to prioritize the objectives. The goal of the roadmap is to address difficulties and uncertainties related to *strategic execution*.

Strategic execution is the most celebrated step in strategy, and is where the forward progress will occur. Many organizations will skip to this step, or only spend time here, which becomes a problem when the lack of strategic context leads to the inability to make the best decisions for the organization.

Of course, there is no way to ensure that the organization is always making the best strategic decisions. The environment will change and it will face new challenges. In order to course correct, organizations must measure their results at regular intervals: *Did the execution affect our current state? Has our future state vision changed? Are there new capabilities we require?* Etc. It is normal to have to make significant shifts in strategic plans as the environment changes within and around the organization. Even shifts in future state vision will be occasionally required. Failure to *iterate* can result in organizations having the wrong target, or maybe missing their mark with respect to what they're trying to accomplish.

THE GREATEST RISK

In the past twenty years, disruption has altered the faces of many industries. No industry seems immune as we've seen hotels, taxis, movies, gaming, long-distance calling, cameras, etc. all upended. Many of the affected companies knew where the source of disruption was coming from, but they lacked the focus, vision, agility, nimbleness, or decisiveness to get the job done themselves.

Very few of the disrupted companies would claim they failed to manage risk effectively. After all, they likely did not fail because of a lawsuit, operational blunder, or single financial misstep. Organizations are successful due in large part to their ability to manage such risks. But the task of risk management seems to have changed faster than organizations could adapt. A mighty adversary has emerged that now threatens traditionally rock-solid organizations, and many are blind to it.

This new threat is *strategic execution risk*, or the risk of not executing on a stated strategy.

A common contributor to strategic execution risk is where the strategy is not well-articulated. I've been part of organizations that thought their strategies were well articulated, but failed to measure whether employees truly understood. Communication must be measured, not just communicated. Strategic articulation should be so clear that any employee, regardless of their role in the organization, understands where the organization is headed. The strategy should be their Eiffel Tower. If you tell them that's where we're headed, they can simply look up and head in that direction.

While strategic articulation issues can easily be overcome, mitigation of strategic execution risk is tricky business. The same tools that are used in other risk management planning efforts can be applied. However, complexity arises when we see that the same measures that are taken to prevent risk in other parts of the organization, are adding to strategic execution risk. Consider a company that has a strategic goal of digitizing its major product lines before the competition beats them to it. In order to execute that strategy, they may need a rapid, major overhaul of their Marketing and Information Technology (IT) departments. This might require immediate layoffs and rapid talent acquisition, which must occur faster than their traditional approaches allow. By the time Human Resources (HR) and Legal have given their opinions on the how the matter should be handled, the competition may have already passed them by.

Prioritizing strategic execution risk mitigation approaches ahead of others requires swift decisions that appear to be high-risk by traditional measures, but are, in effect, risk-mitigating in that they reduce strategic execution risk. For instance, if the potential cost of not executing is greater than the cost of not dotting *i*'s and crossing *t*'s on human resource practices, the traditional HR rules must be broken. Executive teams must be willing to make such trade-offs to advance the organization.

It also requires a realization that decision-making is complex, not linear. Most traditional risk mitigating policies seem linear. That is, action A leads to outcome B. For example, if a legal review is required of each and every HR matter (A), it will reduce legal risk (B). There are so many of these seemingly linear rules in corporate America that decision-makers become complacent. Some may believe these to be the best rules for the organization, regardless of circumstance. However, decision makers should be valued not for their ability to enforce or implement linear risk mitigation policies, but rather for their ability to recognize where the situations are complex, and to take action despite the added complexity.

After all, the decision to not act is still a decision. In this case, the decision to allow traditional risk mitigation measures to delay or trump a measure that mitigates strategic execution risk is also, in fact, a decision. And it's a poor decision: one that can prevent an organization from transforming to what it needs to become before it's too late.

CHAPTER 6: ROLE OF TODAY'S INNOVATOR IN STRATEGY

Recall, we have defined innovation as *the core organizational competency for dealing with the everyday, aggressive pace of change.* Further, we have asserted that many organizations that declare innovation a priority can at least envision a scenario in which they are not likely to achieve some important objective, thus justifying an investment in innovation as a remedy.

Unfortunately, for many organizations, innovation strategy development begins and ends with the declaration of innovation as a priority. As Today's Innovator, you can be left not understanding which direction to head, or even worse, feeling completely rudderless as you wait for direction that may never come. However, it is precisely in these uncertain waters that, if well-prepared, you have the opportunity to establish yourself as a thought leader, helping to inspire a shared vision of what the organization is trying to accomplish and setting clear expectations for others on what role innovation will play in that quest.

It may be the case that the innovation leader, or the innovation team, or the innovation department, is not privy to the highest-level strategic discussions that are taking place within an organization. This is most common in the Dysfunctional or Tentative Maturity Stages, where innovation tends to be separate from, or a bolt-on to, the core strategy. In such cases, it's imperative that you make every effort to insert yourself into the strategic dialog. At the very least, you must attempt to seek out a trusted advisor within the executive ranks who can provide context for any strategic directives that come out. For if you, as Today's Innovator, cannot answer the critical question, "What does the organization require of innovation to achieve its vision?", then it is likely there are many varying perspectives on innovation's role. It is difficult for innovation efforts to meet anyone's expectations in such an environment.

Even if you successfully negotiate your way into the boardroom where the strategy is being formed, you must maintain a broad, open-minded perspective of the organization, and what challenges and opportunities it might be facing. It can be a fatal error for leaders or innovators to be anchored to the belief that they must achieve some certain outcome if the organization doesn't require that outcome to be met, or if the organization is currently unable to achieve such an outcome. Further, it is not enough to roll out a vision statement without rolling up sleeves and doing the dirty work of precisely understanding the "how?" Visions and strategies will always start as just words on paper. An honest strategic assessment is required to determine what it would take to attain the vision. Only by looking from the bird's-eye or balcony view can all of the aspects of the organization be appreciated, respected, and considered. After all, if your organization doesn't currently have the potential to achieve what you're asking it to, you shouldn't expect to achieve it without building new capabilities or making difficult decisions along the way.

If *strategy* is the aim of transforming an organization from what it is today, to what it needs to become (before it's too late), it goes without saying that we must have a great understanding of what the organization is today, and what it is capable of. In cases where the organization's vision might be wildly aspirational, or quite a distance from its current state, it may be required to completely transform the organization and how it operates, in order to reach your destination. In many cases, it is the role of you as Today's Innovator to be the catalyst for the bold, transformational steps that the organization may otherwise be slow to make. If innovation is seen as the remedy, then at least in the back of the leaders' minds there is some expectation that the innovators must take a different approach than that which has set the organization off track. While the innovation program may have been initiated in order to simply execute on a new business idea, it is the most likely place from which new ways of working will rise as the innovation competency is developed.

THE CASE FOR INNOVATION

If you have been assigned the task of innovating or executing on a new business idea, but not the task of building and nurturing an innovation competency, all is not lost. It's a win that the innovation conversation has begun and some resources (at the very least, *you*) have been assigned at all. In this situation, the misguided innovator inside the Dysfunctional Maturity organization would likely begin with an ideation session (post-it notes and easels) — a common misstep that, without luck, will lead to the innovation outcomes failing to meet some unrealistic or unstated expectation.

To ensure that the innovation efforts begin on the right foot, it's important for you to not lead with "ideas." As Today's Innovator, you must first build a strong *case for innovation* that aligns all of the organization's leaders to what they can expect to gain from innovation. This step may seem unnecessary if the innovation imperative has already been declared, but its purpose is less about revisiting the declaration, and more about orienting the organization towards some common expectations. This business case may be the tool that inspires the shift of an organization away from the mindset of "innovation as an outcome," to a competency essential for sustained success.

The case for innovation will essentially act as project plan for building the innovation competency in the organization. Ideally, it should be assembled before the program is launched, or in the program's infancy. Once agreed upon, the case for innovation can morph into the roadmap for the *innovation strategy*, which we'll cover later.

Some key components of such an initial case for innovation include:

1. Overview/restatement of the organization's current state and future state vision

2. Identification of the strategic vectors/priorities for which innovation will play a role

3. Statement of the benefits of developing innovation as a competency

4. Acknowledging the unknowns

5. Establishing initial success measures and milestones

6. Setting the initial innovation investment level

7. Establishing the cadence for innovation strategy iterations

The first two components exist to establish the overall strategic context for innovation. If you have been in the room where this strategic planning has been happening, this should be straightforward. Otherwise, you may structure these components as a dialog to gain agreement amongst the decision-makers on why innovation is required. The third component begins to establish that innovation is not an activity, or an outcome, but rather what is truly being proposed is innovation is a competency that is being built — one that will benefit the organization strategically, but may also have benefits, such as improving corporate culture, enhancing customer experiences, exposing employees to new skills, etc. Again, you can structure this as a dialog to get the decision-makers to contribute their own ideas as to what the benefits might be. The fourth and fifth components acknowledge there are a set of unknowns that still need to be answered, and that answering these unknowns will be the initial success measures and milestones. This may include who is being asked to innovate, where they will innovate, whether consultants will be hired, what training is required, what processes will be used, etc. The sixth component is the initial ask for an innovation budget, which may include salary costs, equipment costs, consultant spending, and more. And the final component sets the cycle, or cadence, for innovation strategy iterations — that is, how frequently you will check back in with executives, how often you will reevaluate change factors, how often you will identify new objectives, etc.

While the precise nature of the initial case for innovation will vary from organization to organization, it's an important step in whatever form it takes. It serves the purpose of setting clear expectations of the innovation program (what it is, and what it is not), in order to reduce the chance that these expectations are not understood later on. However, it is just an initial case. When first assembled, it may be too early to truly know what's expected of innovation for the organization to achieve its objectives. Development of an *innovation strategy* can go a long way towards answering that critical question.

CHAPTER 7: INNOVATION STRATEGY DEVELOPMENT

The development of an *innovation strategy* is not the same exercise as the development of an overall strategy for the organization. It is (usually) a subset of the overall strategy. For instance, an organization may develop both a core business strategy and an innovation strategy, which together, comprise the overall business strategy. Until the point at which the organization has attained Competent Mastery of innovation, the development of a separate innovation strategy is necessary to focus the innovation resources.

In order to develop an innovation strategy, Today's Innovator should follow the same strategy development steps outlined above, beginning with a current state assessment. The difference is your assessment should, obviously, be focused on *innovation*.

A great tool for beginning to understand the current state of the organization with respect to innovation, in particular, is to analyze the *innovation ecosystem*. This is simply the development of a narrative on how innovation is accomplished in your organization today, built by interviewing those who know how to "get things done" in the current environment: executives, product managers, engineers, project managers, etc. It will uncover all of the back-channels, political structures, and organizational standards that must be negotiated to innovate in your organization. These resources should be asked about what pressures they face as they innovate, what they believe is expected of them, and what tools and systems they use (or avoid) in their work. We'll cover the *innovation ecosystem* in much more detail in *Systems of Innovation*.

Next, it may be useful to conduct an exercise of identifying the current, in-flight innovation projects, to understand what innovation is currently on track to contribute financially. This could be an assessment of just the initiatives being worked by dedicated innovation resources, or it can be a broader, organization-wide view. Either way, the goal is to understand whether innovation is on track to deliver what's expected of it.

The first time such a financial outlook is put together for innovation, it will likely be an organization-wide view of innovation, since there may be not yet be any initiatives unique to the innovation program. It's likely for a Dysfunctional Maturity organization that many of these in-flight projects or initiatives will be short-term and related to defending or improving the organization's core. A long-term forecast of financial metrics that your organization tracks closely can then be created by summing up the projected contributions from this innovation portfolio. This will often reveal a financial gap between what's projected and the goal the organization has set. That gap is precisely the gap that innovation needs to address!

If you happen to learn in this exercise that your organization is currently on track to meet its *financial* objectives, then the answer to Critical Question #1 (*What role does innovation play?*) will lie well beyond the financials. Perhaps the role of innovation is to transform the organization to some new vision of what it is trying to become, by entering new markets or exploring new technologies. Or, perhaps you will be one of the lucky few who innovates, simply to explore new frontiers, to accelerate a company's growth, or to accentuate its (already innovative) culture.

After the financial outlook is understood, next conduct an analysis of all of the change factors that your organization faces. This exercise may have been conducted during the overall strategic planning cycle, but it might be useful to conduct an innovation-specific analysis. For instance, consider the case of Apple, who must order a next generation iPhone's hardware to a set of specifications, often before the technology to achieve those specifications even exists! They must reasonably believe that technology will be developed, but also be prepared for the very real possibility that their specifications were either too conservative or too aggressive, then have a plan in place to deal with that situation. This is a change factor that may not be considered in Apple's overall strategy, but is important to those who are innovating the iPhone.

There may be other exercises you should conduct to thoroughly assess your current state, and we'll consider some of those in *Culture of Innovation* to come. There is no right or wrong approach. What's important is that you come out with an understanding of your starting point: what works today, what doesn't, what you're up against, what's in your favor, etc. so that you can create an innovation strategy that improves your innovation competency to deliver what's expected.

The next step in developing the innovation strategy is to compare the current state, with respect to innovation, to the organization's future state vision to begin to understand which strategic priorities or strategic vectors innovation will play a role in. For Dysfunctional or Tentative Maturity organizations, it may be the case that "Innovation" shows up as its own strategic priority. While that is acceptable for some organizations, it does not let the innovators off the hook for developing a detailed innovation strategy.

To review, *strategy* should answer the question of, "How will the organization achieve its vision?" It is the exercise of determining how the organization will bring its future state vision into existence. If the future state vision is aspirational enough, the answer will not be clear, but *it will be discoverable* as the organization makes progress towards the goal.

This strategy will likely consist of a blend of a core strategy with an *innovation strategy*. The core strategy should be focused on change factors affecting the core operations (e.g. to increase sales, to improve quality, to improve customer experience, or to launch a product line extension). The innovation strategy should be focused on change factors which requires exploration and experimentation to extend beyond the capabilities of the organization today. Strategic objectives that can be achieved with current capabilities and current insights should fit squarely into the core strategy. Strategic vectors for which the ultimate outcomes are not yet known, or strategic objectives which require new capabilities or new insight, should be addressed in the *innovation strategy.*

At one of my previous employers, we made the distinction between Customer Experience 2.0 and Customer Experience 3.0. Customer Experience 2.0 was a strategic vector that described what the core business resources should focus on building, whereas Customer Experience 3.0 was an innovation-specific strategic vector to evaluate what the company could transform into in the future. It was the role of Marketing to lead the development of Customer Experience 2.0, and the role of the Innovation Lab Team and R&D to explore the possibilities of Customer Experience 3.0.

Your innovation strategy will likely be comprised of a blend of short-term and long-term strategic objectives, spanning varying types of innovation, such as product innovation, business model innovation, operational innovation, etc. The objectives can be further categorized using an appropriate *innovation portfolio* classification scheme. Pick one that's useful to your organization (e.g. "three horizons" or "core vs. opportunistic vs. breakthrough" or a consultant-built 2x2 matrix). Some of the objectives may be strategically *imperative*, such as developing and deploying new technology platforms. Others may be *conceptual*, such as lab experiments to address or identify unmet needs for a specific consumer segment. Still others may be *experimental*, such as tinkering with or deploying small tech/science advancements. Whatever classification schemes you use, labels should fit the way that project and resource decisions are made in order to prioritize and resource-balance them appropriately.

_____

To identify the new capabilities required to achieve the future state vision, consider the following questions:

1. What new capabilities are required to produce the outcomes we expect to produce?

2. In what ways are we likely to fail in bringing the future state into existence? (Addressing these will help identify new capability requirements)

3. Do we have the right people, talents, technology, platforms, governance systems, etc. to deliver what we need to deliver?

4. What must we STOP doing in order to free up the resources required to execute?

5. How will capability development be funded?

To identify the insights required to achieve the future state vision, consider the following questions:

1. In what ways is the competitive landscape changing?

2. In what ways are consumer preferences likely to change?

3. Are there new rules or regulations which may change the way we do business?

4. What new technologies, startups, and competitors are likely to emerge? Where will they come from?

5. What must we know for sure before we make the next big resource investment?

To define and prioritize the set of strategic initiatives, or outcomes, that will take the organization from its current state to its future state, consider the following questions:

1. What outcomes must occur, and by when?

2. What milestones can be measured along the way?

3. How well do our initiatives align with the strategic vectors we've identified, such as digitalization, or automation?

4. What do we expect to learn from the outcomes and milestones we've defined?

5. How long might it take to achieve the milestones we've identified? What resources are required?

As with the overall strategy, it is important that the innovation strategy development process is not a one-time process. It is decidedly iterative, for as new insights are gained and as new capabilities are unlocked, the path to the future state can and should, change. In fact, it may be required to iterate the innovation strategy more frequently than the overall strategy, since it is likely that the innovation environment is more volatile. Further, the organization may require the development of multiple innovation strategies, focused on various strategic vectors or cascading to lower levels of the organization. What's important is to not get locked in a particular approach *because that's the way things are done*, but instead be willing to change the status quo when the conditions require it.

There exists one serious implication of "innovation as a remedy" that often goes unconsidered and unspoken, namely that if the organization is not meeting its objectives, it's likely that it's because the innovation competency is not well-developed. Restated: innovation is to blame if the organization is missing its mark. There certainly could be other factors, but generally those are known and quantifiable — anything unquantifiable is due to the organization's inability to keep pace with the everyday, aggressive pace of change. This is what I refer to as "The Ultimate Scorecard" for innovation: if the organization, as a whole, is not on track to achieve its objectives, innovation is not producing what the organization requires. As Today's Innovator, you must accept responsibility to shift the innovation strategy accordingly to get the entire organization back on track. Sure, the CEO is ultimately accountable, but you will often have a better vantage point for observing where the innovation efforts are insufficient. Frequently, innovation efforts fail to get the organization back on track because they are too narrow in focus, pointed at just one or a few possible innovation types, such as product innovation or technology innovation. The innovation competency, in such a case, is not being broadly built to extend into other innovation types, such as culture innovation or business model innovation.

CHAPTER 8: ROADMAP, EXECUTION, & ITERATION

BUILDING YOUR ROADMAP

Once the strategic priorities and vectors are identified and you have begun to answer the questions of what capabilities, insights, and outcomes are required, you can create an *innovation strategy roadmap* to follow, in order to make progress towards the vision. The purpose of the roadmap is to get the entire organization to understand and agree with where you are going, how you are going to get there, who is involved, and maybe what tradeoffs are required. Understand that the further out you are looking, the less likely you are to know which new change factors will present themselves. In some instances the roadmap will not be much more effective than a compass, but is better than having no plan at all.

For innovation, the roadmap can be an extension of the initial case for innovation discussed previously. To the extent that the case for innovation considers the *why* of innovation, the roadmap should address the *what* and *how*. It may be wasted energy to build the roadmap if there is not agreement and commitment to the case for innovation from stakeholders, such as the executive team, strategy leaders, business leaders, and innovation resources. However, as Today's Innovator you should have the roadmap-building exercise in mind while building the case for innovation, as it's likely that the organization is in a hurry to see results from innovation efforts. Building these tools in parallel can save you precious time.

As an extension of the case for innovation, the roadmap should recap the elements which have been agreed upon, then go much deeper to detail both *what* must be decided or executed (and by when), as well as *how* the innovation strategy will be executed, including what criteria are to be considered in the decision-making process (for more on *screening criteria*, see *Decision-Making Structures* in *Part 3: Systems of Innovation*). It's important to acknowledge with all stakeholders and innovation resources that the roadmap is a living and breathing document that will change as new insight is gained or as the environment changes. This reduces the pressure to be "right" with the initial roadmap and, instead, allows for creative exploration and experimentation to arrive at a set of objectives or a new decision framework that improves your odds of success. Your roadmap may contain a great place to catalog the many unanswered questions you have that may become answerable at some later date. Below are some of the key elements of the innovation strategy roadmap. We will cover many of these topics in detail in *The Innovation System*.

» Recap of the case for innovation

» Detail on strategic objectives (Insights, Capabilities, and Out-comes)

» Note: this can be classified as your "Innovation Portfolio" and the individual initiatives categorized into an appropriate classification scheme

» Roles and responsibilities for execution

» Innovation governance structure (Decisions, Budget, Projects, Re-sources, Reporting, etc.)

» Budget

» Design of the innovation ecosystem, including:

  » Physical environment

  » Organization scheme

  » Processes & methods utilized

  » Development platforms (Technology/Architecture/Machinery/Application Stacks/etc.)

> » Internal stakeholders

> » External vendors & partners

> » Communication plan

» Input and output metrics

In some cases, it may be necessary to create multiple roadmaps, such as for various innovation types, which might require substantially different approaches, but be sure to keep an overall innovation strategy roadmap as an official document of record on what innovation is accountable for and how it operates.

STRATEGY EXECUTION

The exercise of defining business and innovation strategy can turn out to be far easier than the exercise of executing the strategy. To execute your plan, you must make a deliberate shift after strategic planning, a shift that requires a different way of working — a different mindset. The difference from what you have planned to what ultimately gets executed is called the *strategy-execution gap*, and it can be sizeable. To have such a gap is completely normal, as long as it doesn't plague the organization. Plans change, roadblocks are encountered, and initiatives often take longer or cost more than anticipated. You must be resilient, yet nimble, to make forward progress in the face of the challenges that strategy execution will present. As Today's Innovator, it is you who must set up the environment to improve the odds of success for execution. Below, we will cover a few of the approaches that you can take to improve your organization's innovation execution competency, including Customer Focus, Technology Readiness, Design Standards, Diversity, Quick Wins, and Future Focus.

CUSTOMER FOCUS

Entire graduate degree programs have been developed around the discipline of customer-centricity, and we will cover some of these in *Part*

3: Systems of Innovation later. For now, it's important to understand that all successful innovation will meet, or satisfy, a customer need or pain point. Of course, that just means that the *end product* — that which is measured and observed in the hands of the *end consumer* — satisfies customer needs. It says nothing of how the innovation came to be. Great ideas can come from anywhere; they don't always start with customer insight. However, it will often be the case that you'll seek new insights that can differentiate your approach to innovation relative to your competitors. This could take the form of analyzing customer needs, or exploring new markets to identify what opportunities exist.

Knowing that the end game is to meet or satisfy customer needs, innovators should immerse themselves in customer insight, or customer knowledge, that informs product or feature design. Customer intimacy is an organizational competency, and the more intimate you are with customers and their needs, the greater the odds of innovation success. Additionally, the easier it is to gain customer insight, the more time you can spend designing and testing product features to satisfy customer needs. Consider the availability of customer intelligence and knowledge when answering the question of what new capabilities are required to produce the outcomes you're expected to produce.

TECHNOLOGY READINESS

Today's Innovators tend to be much more successful with strategic execution if the organization has systems and technologies which are ready to be built upon. Technology resources can be incredibly scarce, and waiting for them to become available only when it is time to execute can be frustrating and counter-productive. Instead, you must partner with your technology resources to develop innovation-friendly systems, platforms, or environments, which limit demand of highly specialized resources to build upon. This can take the form of development of dedicated innovation labs, which mimic, or are well integrated into, the organization's systems. This can also take the form of rapid testing and deployment capabilities such as test kitchens, software "sandboxes," or virtual environments. It is likely that development of many of these capabilities will become your strategic objectives, themselves.

To go one step further, innovators will save re-work and headaches downline by innovating with a target technology architecture, such as an application stack, in mind. The more intimately you know the technologies and standards that are used, the easier it will be to integrate innovation back into the organization.

DESIGN STANDARDS

Another method for improving odds of innovation success is developing design standards, which produce interchangeable parts, allow for rapid experimentation, and fit customer expectations of your brand. An example of such standards might be Customer Experience design standards, which promote consistent customer experiences from one product to the next within a brand's product portfolio. When you are acutely aware of standards the organization uses to build products and experiences, you can work within those standards to accelerate your decision-making. I'm not suggesting it should be a rule to *follow* all design standards, for many great innovations arise from simple tweaks of current standards. Instead, making conscious decisions around where to adopt standards, and where not to, can spur creativity and allow you to isolate which tweaks might produce a surprising result. Consider the National Football League's recent addition of a "green zone" graphic which illustrates the distance a team must advance to attain a first down. The standard for several decades has been the use of a graphical yellow line showing the line-to-gain. The simple tweak of adding the "green zone" allows viewers to quickly assess whether the ball carrier has advanced past the line-to-gain, even if that line is not visible in the frame.

DIVERSITY

Workplace diversity is more than just a buzzword. Diverse innovation teams will benefit from varying skill sets and expertise that are key ingredients in creating new products, features, or offerings. Building teams with gender, cultural, and age diversity, will likely expose all team members to different ways of thinking about business problems, and give the teams an extremely broad base of experiences to draw from as they execute.

QUICK WINS

You're likely to hear at the outset of new innovation initiatives that, "We just need a few quick wins." While this seems like it might be an optical maneuver to demonstrate that innovation is working, quick wins can have an impact beyond just looking good. For one, they allow accelerated insights to develop. Further, the process of putting quick wins into market, whether they "win" or not, can uncover inefficiencies or roadblocks to execution that may have otherwise gone unnoticed.

FUTURE FOCUS

Some of the best assets of an organization tend to be hidden in plain sight. By simply reframing the perspective of these assets, incredible innovation potential can be unlocked. For instance, maybe your business has a set of shared service resources, which help the business monitor quality. A shift in focus from simply monitoring quality, to anticipating quality issues of new business models or technologies can mitigate emerging issues before they appear. Similarly, maybe your business has an insights function that produces reports describing products or experiences, such as customer satisfaction surveys. What if, instead of being descriptive, their function was reframed to generate insights that could drive business growth? This act of simply redirecting assets from addressing the business of today, to addressing the business of tomorrow can motivate employees as they engage with innovation efforts. It's not a stretch to believe they could automate or rationalize some of their current-state functions to become more future-focused. Remember to ask: *What does the organization require from my team in order to achieve its vision?*

ITERATION/THE CADENCE

In most organizations today, the demand for innovation is significant. Once that demand has been met, it is often followed by a demand for better communication and faster speed of innovation. Both of these demands can be satisfied with a well-considered *innovation strategy cadence*, or the period of time between strategy planning cycles.

The cycle, itself, is straightforward and, again, consists of the following five steps: Current State Assessment, Future State Assessment, Roadmap Development, Execution, and Iteration.

It may be the case that the cadence varies as the environment changes, and that is acceptable as long as steps are not being inadvertently skipped. In the Insights & Innovation department I led, we developed an innovation strategy cadence, which repeated every six months. Vision and strategy development work tended to be completed just before mid-year, and again just before year-end. Innovation roadmap development work was then completed at mid-year and again by end of year. Project execution tended to follow either quarterly or half-year schedules. The insights, new capabilities, and outcomes from the execution phase would change the current state, and thereby inform the next iteration of the vision, strategy, and roadmap. The advantage of this cadence was that it fit within the already well-established structure of Quarterly Business Reviews (QBRs) that informed so many of the company's higher-level strategic decisions. The end of the first and third quarter reviews were mainly comprised of progress reporting. The end of the second and fourth quarter reviews articulated the vision, strategy or roadmap changes we would be implementing. Further, to build these QBR documents we simply reused elements of our roadmap, which allowed us to reinforce our roadmap with interested stakeholders.

However, in some organizations it may be possible and desirable to shorten the strategy cadence to coincide with agile "sprints," often as short as two weeks. Annual cycles may make sense for other organizations. What's important is that A) steps are not inadvertently skipped, B) that the information that needs to be communicated to the various stakeholders is shared, and C) that the organization is learning, adapting, and continuously improving at each iteration. It may be the case that strategic pivots will occur at the various development and decision points, and it's important that the organization is prepared for and told about those pivots.

Innovators should work with stakeholders to define the milestones they expect to reach along the way, understanding that the closer the milestone is, the more likely it is to be hit. Further out milestones, maybe a year or more into the future, may never be attained as the environment will evolve rapidly as you make progress. This exercise gives innovation teams clear direction and sets them up for success to meet the organization's expectations. In the absence of this milestone framework, innovators tend to either get stuck on ideation or *front-end* innovation exercises, or they fail to communicate progress as they become unsure of what's important to communicate.

Some organizations find that their innovation strategy iterations may follow waves, themes, or natural progressions. For instance, maybe a first wave focused on Technology Readiness is followed by a second focused on Customer Insight, and a third focused on Quick Wins. The exercise of labeling these waves can be important for establishing common language and priorities within the group that is innovating, and to make sure that outside stakeholders know what to expect from each of the waves.

One of the biggest challenges with such a cadence is that innovators must learn to effectively toggle between the strategic focus of bringing the future state vision into existence and the execution focus of completing objectives at hand. When tasks are completed, or experiments are conducted, or capabilities are acquired, you can then build upon the insight or capability to chain together a progressive set of outcomes that form a path to attaining the future state.

CHAPTER 9: INNOVATION MATURITY STAGES: STRATEGIC MATURITY

Now that we've had a chance to establish the role of *The Innovation Strategy* in an organization, we can quickly revisit the Maturity Stages to further illustrate how organizations in the various stages might differ.

DYSFUNCTIONAL MATURITY STAGE

Dysfunctional Maturity organizations have failed to establish foundational elements of the case for innovation, such as a future state vision. Innovation initiatives may fail to fit into broader strategic context. Often, it's unclear where the budget or execution resources for innovation will come from. The status quo of the organization is likely to persist, unaware and unaffected by a compelling case for change.

TENTATIVE MATURITY STAGE

Here, organizations are talking about continuing to execute their core strategy, *and* innovating. Innovation likely has its own strategy, independent of the strategic priorities of the organization. It is not clear how any trade-offs will be made when these efforts inevitably compete for resources. Innovation may feel like an experiment, with a team carved out to work on innovation, maybe off-site or in a special room set aside for innovation. The organization is trying to closely manage predictable shifts in its status quo.

CONFIDENT MATURITY STAGE

Confident organizations have begun to establish the importance of innovation to the overall strategy, and the innovation strategy has become well-defined. The budget and resources are established, but innovation initiatives must still compete for resources, particularly when trying to embed new products or technologies back into the core. By reinforcing the importance of innovation relative to change factors, the status quo of the organization is actively being upset; it is changing.

COMPETENT MASTERY STAGE

As we established before, for Competent Masters of innovation, the innovation strategy is indiscernible from the core strategy; having a separate innovation strategy is not necessary. Innovation is always on. It has become essential to and embedded within the organization. It is no longer separate from, or ancillary, to the strategy. Rather, innovation is the strategy. The status quo is continuously transforming.

CHAPTER 10: RESISTANCE & ROADBLOCKS OF THE INNOVATION STRATEGY

As Today's Innovator, you must become both the strategist and the practitioner, clear about where the organization is headed and how the various insights gained will get it there. Training an organization to integrate sound innovation strategy planning into its core operations is a challenge. It can feel scary, particularly as the maturation process produces a corresponding values shift from *persistence* and *predictability,* to *change* and *transformation.* In the next part, *Culture of Innovation,* we'll apply this same planning framework to an organization's culture so that such values shifts are planned, designed, and expected. But first, let's identify some common roadblocks or modes of resistance you might encounter while developing and executing an innovation strategy.

ABSENCE OF VISION

Innovation can be accomplished in the absence of a shared vision amongst the stakeholders, but it's analogous to trying to design a perfect piece of art for a buyer, without understanding what the buyer's preferences are or where they're planning to display the art. The more you know about the buyer's style, tastes, and expectations, the more likely you are to meet their expectations. Organizations that initiate innovation without making clear where the organization is headed are setting their innovators up for failure. Stakeholders will have varying expectations of what the innovators should produce, and for what reason. This may ultimately lead to lack of institutional support for the innovators, making their job even more challenging. It is far more likely that the innovators will disappoint most stakeholders, rather than please most of them. Today's Innovator should work with the stakeholders (executives, business leaders, customers, etc.) to develop a shared vision for the organization and to define innovation's role in achieving that vision.

INSUFFICIENT STRATEGIC COMMUNICATIONS

It will not suffice to create a shared future state vision and corresponding strategy, without a plan to communicate the vision and strategy broadly. Unfortunately, many organizations neglect to pay adequate attention to strategic communications, which leaves unaddressed questions about the vision or strategy in the heads of those who are expected to execute. There are several forms that inadequate communications might take, including using language or concepts that are foreign to the intended audience, limiting the frequency of communication, limiting the strategic context included in the communication, limiting the amount of discourse around the strategy, or not clearly expressing in what ways the organization could, should, or will *change*. Any of these factors can leave the organization chasing out-of-date goals, or cause innovators to appear unfocused or ineffective. Executives may feel like there is active resistance to the new vision or strategy. However, that may simply be because *lack of clarity looks like resistance*. Restated: if any in the organization is unclear how they should respond to new direction, managers may misconstrue that lack of clarity for active resistance. In reality, some time spent on establishing appropriate context, discourse, and expectations will pay off. While there is no "right" way to communicate strategically, the effectiveness can always be measured to determine whether the organization understands what's now expected of them.

LACK OF INNOVATION BRAND

When first introduced to an organization, *innovation* can mean different things to many different people. This can lead to varying expectations among stakeholders as to what innovation's role is. Some may view the innovators as the people who "play all day," others may think that the innovators should be producing new products, others may wonder what the innovators have accomplished, and still others may not be aware that the organization has put innovation in motion. The best way to deal with such misconceptions is by actively branding the organization's innovation activities. This involves establishing a robust communication plan, or marketing plan, for innovation, including both internal and external components. Internally, the communication plan may include product or team launch announcements, it may feature business leaders speaking on the role of innovation in team or department meetings, it may establish best-practice-sharing and story-telling procedures for innovators, etc. Externally, the communication plan of innovation may be multi-faceted as well. It might involve brand-enrichment, such as what Nissan or the human resources company Workday have done to integrate innovation into their brand messaging. It might involve the build of an innovation website to engage customers, such as what Starbucks has created at https://ideas.starbucks.com. It might involve public relations announcements around product launches, such as what Apple does with new iPhone versions. Or, maybe the organization encourages its innovators to become industry conference speakers.

The content of these communications can include quick wins, big wins, thought leadership platforms, new ventures/partnership announcements, and much more. For organizations who have become Competent Masters of innovation, innovation becomes a common thread within nearly all communications, rather than a separate, bolted-on marketing or communication plan. That way it's not treated as something exceptional to the organization and its value set, and instead, is communicated as essential to the strategy and value set of the organization.

CORE VS. INNOVATION: ORGAN REJECTION

In organizations that have not yet established Competent Mastery of innovation, there will be a natural divide between new, innovative objectives and core, or traditional, objectives. This divide will likely be reinforced as the organization takes care to separate the innovation activity from the core business activity — either physically, or organizationally, or both. While this divide is not inherently bad, it can cause the core of the organization to resent the innovation efforts, particularly when they are unclear as to the role that innovation is playing in helping the organization achieve its vision. Further, the core is likely very good at what it does, which is why it has become the "core." But, as a result, this implies that it is very good at not doing what it doesn't do. That is, *the gravity of the status quo is strong.* Every process, procedure, rule, resource, and decision has been put in place to make sure the core continues to do what it does. When innovation is introduced, by definition it threatens the status quo. The very rules and habits that govern the activities of the organization today, will become the same structures that prevent innovation from flourishing inside the organization. As Today's Innovator you must understand and appreciate the rules and procedures that govern the organization's core operations. It is up to you to fight to overcome the resistance that will be presented, or risk "organ rejection" as innovations fail to integrate into the core. You may produce the next $60 billion product, but if the core is not ready to integrate that product and change its business model accordingly, the innovation may be snuffed out before it has a chance to thrive.

Consider Kodak, who by many accounts invented digital photography. However, their core film-based photography business was not nimble enough to adapt to the changes that digital photography demanded. Eventually, competitors flooded the digital camera market with new, high-tech equipment, and Instagram rose to prominence as a medium for storing and exchanging digital photos, which made Kodak all but obsolete.

UNAWARENESS OF COMPETITION, STARTUPS, & ADJACENT INDUSTRIES

As the demands of complex organizations intensify from increased regulation, declining product performance, or any other change factor commonly seen today, it is easy for even the savviest innovator to face organizationally *inward* to fight the fires that these pressures create. While intense focus on such pressures and issues can produce valuable and deep expertise, it is often at the expense of broad perspective for how the world is changing outside the organization's four walls. It is your role as Today's Innovator to stay on top of competitive intelligence, the startup environment, as well as adjacent industries, which might start to overlap or threaten your organization. Failure to face *outward* could cause you to overlook a trend, a technology, an emerging science, or an opportunity to partner with or acquire a business that could have propelled the company forward towards its vision.

* * *

The importance of setting a compelling, aspirational, and attainable vision and a corresponding strategy cannot be understated. Organizations must understand the waters that they're navigating, and have their sights set on a vision that may be quite unknown today. But their focus cannot solely be on the horizon, for if there is mutiny within the crew, they will for sure never reach their destination.

PART 2: CULTURE OF INNOVATION

Culture is not the most important thing in the world. It's the only thing.

-Jim Sinegal, Costco CEO

The recruiter stated it clearly enough, "Identifying and solving business problems."

His reply had been in response to a rather direct question of mine. I had asked, "What behaviors get people promoted?" He didn't even have to think about it.

Identifying and solving business problems. What I soon learned was that this "recruiter," who I'd believed was a human resources employee, was actually a high-performing business leader who was taking a genuine interest in the talent the company was hiring out of college. If I hadn't sought him out after accepting the job, I maybe would have never seen him again. He wasn't hiring someone for *his team.* He was recruiting someone for the company, screening dozens of candidates for the one or two who would be a fit with the company's values.

This was Capital One in the late 1990s. They were hiring so fast that many of their departments would double in number of employees each year, and the hiring still wasn't fast enough to meet the demand. This credit card company wasn't looking for candidates with five years of experience, or with an M.B.A., or even with interest in financial services. They were looking for engineers, statisticians, mathematicians — those who could identify and solve business problems in new frontiers of marketing and data-driven decision-making.

New hires were brought into an environment where they were challenged from day one to think critically, to break down barriers, to get better every day, to experiment, and to upset the status quo. These behaviors were reinforced, not by banners on the walls or mass emails, but by the culture itself. Though they did not call it that, Capital One had built a "Culture of Innovation" from scratch. Each employee felt a duty to hold the other employees accountable to the culture that would allow this company to grow from a two-employee spin-off of a traditional bank in 1994, to one of the biggest credit card companies in the world. Ultimately, it would become a rock-solid bank with a Competent Mastery of innovation, which would rather easily withstand the Global Financial Crisis of 2008.

* * *

You may recall from *Part 1: The Innovation Strategy* that there are strong arguments on both sides for whether it is more important to first build a supportive work culture or a sound innovation strategy. I stated there that it would be a challenge to attempt to design and change a culture without a clear understanding of what it is you are expected to accomplish, namely, the *strategy.*

While that may be true, as equally challenging might be to try to execute on an innovation strategy without a deep-rooted foundation of values that support the innovation competency. When organizations declare innovation a priority, many will neglect to design the supportive cultural environment that allows for new ideas, new products, new technologies, and new business models to emerge and mature. In the absence of such a culture, innovators will find it a challenge to be creative enough, or collaborative enough, or clever enough, or just obedient enough to find success.

In this part, we will explore how to design and implement a Culture of Innovation, which sets Today's Innovators up for success, beginning with a *Culture Primer*: a level-setting overview of *culture* to develop common language and to explore how culture can affect an organization. We'll then look at your *Role as Today's Innovator* in driving culture change in your team and organization, using the same process you would use to design and execute an innovation strategy. We'll cover best practices in *Developing Your Culture Change Program,* as well as how to build a *Roadmap for Execution and Iteration.* Finally, we'll look at how culture might appear in the various *Innovation Maturity Stages* and consider how to overcome some likely sources of *Resistance and Roadblocks.*

CHAPTER 11: A CULTURE PRIMER

Culture is easy to feel, but difficult to explain. In order to design a high-performance innovation culture, however, you must begin by understanding what your organization's current culture is, as well as how it operates. This starts by *describing* the observable events and behaviors that occur in a workplace culture, then *diagnosing* what structures, assumptions, and values cause those events and behaviors to occur and recur.

Describing your team's or organization's culture is straightforward, it's simply the exercise of measuring the observable actions, events, stories, and behaviors that employees exhibit, then identifying which of these cultural traits are working well and which are not. Some traits will be readily apparent. Upon close inspection or inquiry, you can likely find some less obvious traits of the culture, such as patterns. For example, maybe the employees' heads are down when doing their work, but very friendly with each other at break time. Maybe there's excitement over an upcoming teambuilding event, but the employees who must stay back to keep the business running don't share the excitement. Or, maybe the CEO keeps talking about being innovative, but, as the employees say, "nothing ever changes."

Diagnosing culture is the exercise of understanding *why* these actions, events, stories and behaviors happen, and why they might continue to happen. Again, in some cases the cause may be obvious, taking the form of rules or structures. Some examples of such rules and structures might be hiring practices, budgets, financial cycles, employee handbooks, organizational structures, building layouts, rewards mechanisms, etc. But if you wish to change the behaviors of a culture, it's important to recognize a change in the rules and structures may not be sufficient to significantly change behavior (e.g. organizational changes, new office layouts, new budget processes, etc.). Many behavioral patterns will be difficult to explain, reinforced by sub-surface forces that are nearly impossible to uncover.

All organizations develop deeply-ingrained habits, or narratives, that continue to reinforce patterns of behavior, regardless of what structure is in place. These habits and narratives are formed over long periods of time, and are based on widely-held, but seldom-surfaced, assumptions. For instance, maybe your marketing team has displayed the pattern of failing to communicate their marketing changes to affected stakeholders. Sure, this may be because marketing is located in some far corner of the building, physically cut off from the other departments, but it also may be reinforced by an underlying belief held by the marketers that they are the pace-setters, and other departments should be able to keep up with what they are doing.

Beyond the habits and narratives, it is the organization's set of *values* that keeps the organization's belief system running. Values direct the standards of behavior within the organization, holding behavioral norms in place. Organizations often state, publicly, a set of values defining how they work. For example, the United States Postal Service has a simple set of stated values: *Trusted, Reliable and Affordable.* Southwest Airlines, as you might expect, has a colorful set of "living values," as they describe them: *Warrior Spirit, Servant's Heart, Fun-LUVing Attitude.* Proctor & Gamble boasts a rather traditional set of corporate stated values: *Integrity, Leadership, Ownership, Passion for Winning, and Trust.*

Sometimes values hang from the ceiling (such as at Initech, the fictitious company in the movie *Office Space*, where a banner hangs over a sea of cubicles that reads: "Initiative + Technology = Initech"). Sometimes they are detailed in employee handbooks, or presented at all-employee meetings. Sometimes they're found on t-shirts and mousepads, presented to employees as gifts or rewards. It's likely that they were very carefully selected after hours, if not days, weeks, or months, of deliberation. Many times, stated values will reflect the identity that a founder or CEO has of herself.

Many organizations will design their stated values directly into the way that they operate. For instance, there may be rewards programs which incentivize people to go above and beyond in customer service. Or, there may be stories on the organization's intranet which feature employees who have shown great integrity or ingenuity. But, this begs the question: If the stated values must be highlighted, then are they truly reflective of the values of the organization? If it were a *real value*, it would be *everywhere*; it would not be exceptional.

Often, an organization's values are unintentional, unspoken, and misunderstood, rooted deep in the organization's cultural core, murky and difficult to discern. An organization's *real values* may vary substantially from the organization's *stated values*. In practice, stated values rarely represent the real values of an organization. A few years back, a presentation called the "Culture Deck" from Netflix suddenly appeared on the scene, showing up in message boards and slide share sites for corporate culture scholars to admire. In this presentation, Netflix asserted that the real values of the organization can be discerned by observing who is getting rewarded, promoted, and let go from an organization. Is it the employee who seemingly works 24 hours a day that gets the promotion? Maybe it's the sales director who just landed the next big contract? Or is it the innovator, or the creative genius, that is celebrated?

An issue further complicating the task of diagnosing the culture, is that it is common for small teams or departments to have different values, different narratives, or different traits than the organization as a whole. In fact, many cultures and subcultures can exist within an organization, often referred to as *silos*. Individual teams may have values that differ from the real or stated values of their business division. Or, varying brands within the same shell company may have different values from one another. The more companies and cultures that exist in the organization, the more difficult it is for anyone to truly understand what the real values might be.

It isn't necessarily a bad thing when organizations work within silos and possess subcultures that govern how each silo operates. Team subcultures can reinforce their own values; members can feel like family and often share common interests and concerns. Further, siloed organizational structures can nurture expertise and focus, and can be a differentiator. In fact, deep expertise can be one of the strongest drivers of successful innovation — the type of expertise that is found in a highly specialized engineering team, for instance. Organizational silos can become problematic when the cultural differences between silos are not well understood, or when a given organizational silo does not engage in a bigger picture cause that others within the same organization expect them to. To the extent that you, as Today's Innovator, are expected to rely upon expert resources found in the far reaches of the organization, you must be acutely aware of these various subcultures. To gain alignment, you will often act as a storyteller to link the narratives of an organizational silo to the broader organizational vision.

The collective set of values, habits, and narratives (the deep-rooted cultural traits), which show up as observable patterns and behavioral norms, comprise the *identity* of a team or organization. To a large extent, even though it is difficult to label, the identity of an organization can be held sacred. As employees learn the acceptable and rewarded behaviors, they begin to understand the rules of the game. And, once the rules are understood, employees don't like the rules to change! Many individuals will establish their own personal identities within the context of their organization's identity. The same is true for national identity, religious identity, or any other cultural identity. It feels good when the beliefs you hold, and when the stories you tell, are well understood, and are common among the people you interact with.

The fact of the matter is that if the status quo were working to deliver on the objectives of the organization, innovation would not be needed. It is your job, as Today's Innovator, to upset the status quo. As soon as the case for innovation is presented, the argument has been made that the status quo must change to produce new and different results. Unfortunately, cultures have a tendency to cling to their identities. To escape this gravity, the *gravity of the status quo*, you must identify and shift the undesirable patterns of behavior which stand in the way of innovation. But because the identity of an organization is complex, and because some of the most deep-rooted traits are unknowable, to produce a consistent shift of behaviors will often require a change to the entire system — from the structures, to the narratives, to its values — in order to take hold.

CHAPTER 12: ROLE OF TODAY'S INNOVATOR IN CULTURE

You may be saying at this point, "It can't really be the role of the *innovator* to change the deep-rooted traits of an organization's culture." This is not traditionally viewed as a job requirement of an innovator. I held the same belief when I first obtained the title of Chief Innovation Officer (CInO). This was my dream job title. I had worked my way through organizational politics, survived and thrived amidst organizational upheaval, and demonstrated a competency for innovating that led me, and others, to believe I'd be successful as the CInO. I had a Master's Degree in Math, deep experience with experimentation, and was marginally more articulate than other quant geeks that might be considered for the role. In retrospect, it is clear that those credentials, while looking good on paper, would not do much to help me succeed.

I began my tenure of CInO believing my job would be to build innovation labs, to install cutting-edge processes, and hire people who think differently, all in order to achieve spectacular innovation. Just a few months in, I was disillusioned. The job was not about fancy labs and new ideas. It did not (yet) require cutting-edge thinking to produce other-worldly results. It was not about innovation as the *outcome*. The job I had received was a *human* one, requiring tolerance, compassion, and empathy. It was about installing innovation, the *competency*, into an organization which was designed to maintain its course — one designed decidedly *not* to adapt and pivot, but rather resist when faced with change factors.

Had I duped myself into believing this was my dream job? The true quest that stood before me was to transform my organization's culture from a traditional, hierarchical culture of compliance — *do what you're told, and don't do what you're not told* — to a "culture of innovation, collaboration, and trust." As it turned out, I would need to scratch and claw, push and prod, day and night, deep below the surface from what could be seen or understood, in order to gain every inch towards becoming an innovative organization. There were many things working against me:

» I had just a team of three people at the outset (myself included) who were being asked to change the culture of 6,000.

» I was not the ideal candidate for the job; I lacked the required empathy for recognizing how the world operated outside of my own little bubble.

» Even with my fancy title, I held no power or sway beyond the influence I'd previously had. There was no magic wand that could be waved that would suddenly give me the power to change deeply entrenched behavioral norms to transform a stuffy company into a dynamic, innovative one.

» I wasn't handed a blueprint, or any sort of plan, when asked to lead the transformation; it was fully expected that I would be able to figure it out.

What I didn't understand at the time was that I was squaring off against the organization's values. In order to become innovative, the entire value system would need to change to become more nimble, agile, and responsive in the face of change. Further, there were few others in the organization who truly were on my side. Even if they wished to help, at the end of the day, their careers (and bonuses) did not directly depend on their ability to shift the culture, unlike mine. Most were busy holding the status quo in place.

Thankfully, I was given the financial resources to hire consultants who had experience with both innovation and culture change. Over the course of several months, we worked together to create a plan for our specific situation (again, there is no single, guaranteed system of success). However, the steps we would take can be described generically, and they may look familiar — it is the same cycle used for executing an innovation strategy:

Step 1: Assess the Current State

Step 2: Articulate the Future State

Step 3: Develop the Roadmap

Step 4: Execute the Plan

Step 5: Iterate

Strangely enough, Today's Innovator is often asked to innovate *because* their value set differs from the rest of the organization. If this sentence describes you, it's important for you to attempt to qualify to what extent your personal values align (or don't align) with those of your organization. You've likely demonstrated a set of personal values which are admirable, but not pervasive, in the organization. This situation can produce a painful values conflict. One way to tolerate a values conflict between you and your organization is to simply acknowledge it. Accept it as a trade-off that you work for an organization whose values conflict with yours. Then, work to change the organization's conflicting values to a set of values that will allow you to be the best version of yourself at work. This isn't always such a clear-cut decision, however; it is one you'll have to live with each day, until it is resolved. For instance, at one of my employers, there was a *real value*, as described to me by many employees, of "keeping your head down and doing your job." On several occasions, I had deep conversations with employees who were distraught by this value. They wanted desperately to speak up and promote change to be more inclusive, creative, collaborative, etc. but were forced to choose between keeping their heads down and risking their career.

If faced with this scenario, you might ask yourself if you are truly in a position of authority or competency to pull out of such a situation. Are you able to drive the change to a more aligned value set? If not, are you willing to make the trade-off to "keep your head down," in order to earn your paycheck? While there is no shame in the latter, it can be stressful and exhausting to conform to the culture's values when they conflict with your own.

It is precisely this difference in values between Today's Innovator and their organization which makes innovation so challenging, and puts them on the front lines of culture change. You will be valued for your ability to think differently, and for this same reason your approach and your ideas will be met with resistance. *For if there is no resistance, you're in the status quo!* It is particularly common in the Dysfunctional or Tentative Maturity Stage that the values of the teams who are innovating may conflict with the values of the broader organization. While the organization may be stating publicly that they value innovation, the real value set may reward a conflicting set of values such as predictability or quality.

Though it may be feasible to fight the resistance in the short-term, your work will become easier if you are able to address the conflicts, to drive the change to a set of innovation-friendly values. At the very least, the innovators, themselves, will need to establish an identity that is well-understood, high-functioning, and common among them. It is likely, as well, that there will be a case to be made to try to shift the identity of the entire organization. Either way, as with setting an innovation strategy, in an effort to align all stakeholders, it is a wise move to initiate any culture change program with a business case that articulates the case for change.

THE CASE FOR CULTURE CHANGE

When leaders expect innovation as an outcome, they may be unaware how difficult it might be to achieve that outcome without cultural change. It will frequently be left to Today's Innovator to create a *case for culture change* in order for a new, innovation-friendly culture to emerge. If your organization's innovation activity is likely to be focused within a fully-dedicated team that is insulated from the core organization, then a broad cultural change program is probably not necessary. However, the core organization's values and narratives may heavily influence the formation of the new culture within the dedicated team, requiring at least some attention be paid to designing and measuring the new team's culture.

The initial case for culture change can take many different forms. It may be developed by Human Resources, it may be developed by an Innovation Team or Employee Experience Team, or it may be feasible to integrate it into the case for innovation as described in *Part 1: The Innovation Strategy*. Whichever form it takes, it's critical you are involved to ensure that the ultimate goal of the change is a culture that is friendly to innovation—or even better, one that *sustains* innovation.

While we will not go into detail on how to build a specific case for culture change document, we will in the next chapters touch upon several of the potential components, which are not dissimilar from the components of the initial case for innovation.

1. Overview/restatement of the organization's current state and future state vision

2. Current state culture hypotheses (or assessment, if available)

3. Statement of the benefits and objectives of culture change

4. Acknowledging the unknowns

5. Establishing initial success measures and milestones

6. Setting the initial culture change investment level/budget

7. Establishing the cadence for culture change program iterations

CHAPTER 13: DEVELOPING YOUR CULTURE CHANGE PROGRAM

Once the case for culture change is assembled and agreed upon, the next step is to assess the current state of the culture. The starting point of *assessing the current state* is not one to be taken lightly. If done correctly, it will expose the team or organization's malignancies, its weaknesses, and its skeletons. It will name names and, as a result, can possibly create resentment of the program from the outset. But, as a trusted coach of mine said of cultural problems, "If you can't name it, you can't fix it." The assessment will serve as a benchmark of the culture you're starting from, allowing you to build a path to get to where you're going, as well as to measure your progress.

To assess, or benchmark, the current state, you must collect data, observe behaviors, and probe to uncover the attitudes and beliefs within the organization, both qualitatively and quantitatively. Then, you must roll up your sleeves to dig into the "whys" of what you find, uncovering the assumptions and narratives that allow the beliefs and behaviors to persist. Through this feedback, you are given hints as to what values might drive the current system to operate the way that it does. Some of the tools you may use to measure and collect feedback include:

» Data from sources such as Human Resources that show patterns of promotion, hiring, terminations, bonuses, etc.

» One-on-one interviews with a cross-section of employees to gain a deep, qualitative perspective on how the culture operates.

» Focus groups with homogeneous sets of employees to hear the language that is used, and the stories told about the culture.

» Employee surveys to gain a quantitative understanding of what traits or characteristics employees associate with the culture.

» Volunteer employee panels who help to explain and complement the findings of any or all of the above.

Even with all of the data you might collect in this benchmarking task, identifying, validating, and measuring the impact of your organization's *real* value set is not simple. But in order to hold the organization accountable to its stated values, this work must be done; it must be understood how values manifest themselves in the observable and measurable culture.

As an innovation leader tasked with driving cultural change, perhaps the most effective tool I found to gain cultural perspective was actively listening. For me, this didn't come easy. As an analytical introvert, the idea of collecting subjective data through conversation was frightening and flew in the face of the data-driven approaches I'd found so successful in my past roles. However, in the end, learning how to talk to a co-worker I'd never spoken with, invite them to lunch, and simply ask them, "how are things going?" ended up yielding incredible insight that I wouldn't have otherwise gained. Listening to what the culture had to say, and how it was said, allowed for added texture and context to the data that would not have been uncovered by other methods.

When uncovering the deep-rooted values and narratives that reinforce your culture's observable behavior, it's important to compare your findings to what you expected to find. Then ask: which values are different from, or missing from, what we have stated our values should be?

While a thorough diagnosis of your organization's real values is a wonderful first step, it's obviously not sufficient, in and of itself, to meaningfully address or change any of the shortcomings identified. A changing team or organization must develop *a future state identity* to move towards.

* * *

One year into my CEO's declaration of innovation (that we would create a culture of innovation, collaboration, and trust), the needle still hadn't moved. No significant innovation was taking place, and the culture remained in place, unchanged by any of the exciting, yet empty, talk of innovation. It was at that one-year point that we had collected enough data and feedback on the current state culture, and we were ready to finally design a compelling vision of how we would like to describe ourselves. This vision was to be a future state identity that addressed the shortcomings of the current culture and would allow innovation to thrive. A meeting was called of the Executive Innovation Team, a hand-selected group of twenty dynamic and concerned leaders from across the company, to get together to design our future state identity. It was at this pivotal meeting that we all gained the first common understanding of what it was we were aiming to accomplish. The collective work of a year's worth of cultural diagnosis converged together at that single point in time to help us develop a vision of a company we would all be extremely proud to work for, one that would be able to reach its potential and achieve things that were currently improbable, at best.

As the Executive Innovation Team compiled its work of designing our future state identity, a near utopian design of our possible future identity began to take shape. Words like *pride, excitement, innovation, teamwork, challenge, rewarding, cutting-edge, industry-leading, desired, pace-setting,* and *empowering* were assembled together to answer the question of what we wanted our future state identity to be. I recall one leader timidly raising her hand, stopping the buzz of energy all around when I called on her. She thought for a while before she spoke, as everyone turned in their chairs to hear what she would say. Her head tilted and she raised her finger and pointed at the screen where we were capturing all of these words. Then, she said, excitedly, "I want to work *there!*" There was a pause, then the room erupted in laughter. It was a memorable moment, for sure, but to this day I'm unclear on why we were laughing. Was it because she was so animated? Or, instead, we were laughing nervously because that possible future state was so far, maybe too far, from what we had diagnosed our current state to be? We had indeed designed a future state in which we all wanted to work, but it was clear that the effort required to get there would be great.

* * *

Only after the current state assessment is complete should you begin to consider what it would take to improve on some of the undesirable traits you've uncovered. Remember, it is your organization's values which hold its behavioral norms in place. Reactively trying to fix the undesirable traits you've uncovered often will not produce the intended result. For the purposes of changing culture, you must develop a plan to move from a set of real and/or stated values to a new set of *aspirational values*. Similar to the future state vision we defined in *Part 1: The Innovation Strategy*, aspirational values are an articulation of some desirable, compelling future state for the organization to work towards. While it may lead to some shame to uncover the real nature of the values at your organization, this can be offset with the pride associated with stating *what we want to become*, and *how we're going to get there*.

In designing your team's or organization's future state identity, some care must be taken to ensure that it is commonly understood, and is truly shared. Further, knowing what you now know about the challenges of the current environment, you must ask: What sustaining values must be instilled in the future state in order to avoid reverting to old habits or patterns? Or, what traits would allow such an environment to persist? In the design of an innovation-friendly environment, you'll need to consider to what extent you will value speed of execution, creativity, excellence, invention, responsiveness, nimbleness, learning, adaptivity, and more. This goes back to the definition of innovation introduced earlier: How will you ensure that this new environment can deal with the everyday, aggressive pace of change that your organization faces? The answer to that question should yield the sustaining traits you must design into your future state identity. For instance, many innovative organizations favor speed and smart failure (or experimentation) over diligence and decision-making by consensus. Be sure to check back in with the stakeholders to ensure there is a common understanding of all of the new words and terms that have been built into the design. Finally, it's important to ensure that this vision is truly *shared*, as shared visions will breed commitment. If there are doubts, or lingering questions, they should be addressed before the vision is articulated to a broader set of stakeholders, such as investors or employees.

CHAPTER 14: ROADMAP, EXECUTION, AND ITERATION

When you are ready to declare the future state shared vision as the identity the organization will strive to attain, the steps to get there will not necessarily be known. The process of developing structures to produce new outcomes is decidedly a test-and-learn process, and it's a process that the organization must be prepared for. You can't reasonably expect change if it's not perfectly clear to those who must change what, precisely, will be expected of them in the new reality. As one of my Executive Innovation Team members described it, think of the employees as swinging on a trapeze. When you ask them to change, you're asking them to let go of the predictable trapeze on which they've grown so comfortable, and instead take hold of a new trapeze, which they may not even yet see in front of them.

BUILDING YOUR ROADMAP

Though the challenges you'll face might be terrific, the *roadmap for culture change* does not have to be overly complex. It's an exercise of understanding the various stages that the organization will pass through on the way to its destination, and what will be expected of each employee along the way. This implies that the change process is just that — a process, or a journey, that the organization will embark on. It is not a switch that can be flipped, where everyone will wake up one day and the entire organization has changed around them. Organizational change requires each and every individual to change within the system. This includes the leaders, the innovators, and the employees.

The stages that a changing organization will pass through are, generally, first *measuring the status quo*, second, progressing to *change readiness*, third, *making change*, and lastly, to *sustaining the change*. When broken down this way, it's clear the actions that the change agents will have to take at each stage along the roadmap are quite different. But don't assume these stages will always progress in this order. As the impact of changes are measured, and as the world continues to change, it may be necessary to step back to evaluating the status quo, or to a new change readiness phase, etc. The purpose of the roadmap is to get the stakeholder to understand and agree with where we are going, how we are going to get there, who is involved, and what tradeoffs are required.

EXECUTING THE CULTURE PROGRAM

Any change program must meet the organization where it is today and take it to where it needs to be, and there are no obvious shortcuts. As with any type of innovation, where the precise steps are unknown, the key lies with improving your odds of success along the way. Here are a few strategies for improving your odds of success in executing your change program.

FOCUS ON HIGHEST-LEVERAGE OPPORTUNITIES

Changing organizations will only have so much bandwidth for designing, implementing, and absorbing the change program. For sure, the great ideas for changing the organization will far exceed the organization's capacity. Care must be taken not to allow pet projects, highly complex initiatives, or efforts which have very little promise for shifting the culture, to take up the bandwidth of the change agents. A fair and balanced approach to evaluating the level of effort against the anticipated outcome can help ensure that only the highest-leverage initiatives are undertaken.

ENGAGE WITH ORGANIZATIONAL VALUES

Only once you've done all the legwork to understand the organization's current value set and to design the future state identity's value set, should you design your transformation program. This program should be focused on transforming your organization's current state values into its future state values, treating each independently. Many aspirational values will require a set of structures to be built that reinforce that particular value. For instance, you may wish to change from an organization which punishes failure (a very real value of many organizations) to one that rewards experimentation. This might involve designing new programs in which employees can learn how to create hypothesis-driven market tests and new forums where they can report on their findings and share what they've learned.

ENLISTING EMPLOYEES IN THE CHANGE PROCESS

You'll recall that I once was part of a team of three employees expected to lead a large culture change program. We were in no way equipped to motivate the organization (with its deeply entrenched value set) to change overnight, if ever. It was clear we couldn't do it alone. Luckily for us, the mere mention of the word "innovation" carried enough mystique, and enough hope, that it was no difficult task to recruit volunteers in the cause of creating a "culture of innovation." In retrospect, having such a lean team at the outset of our program allowed us the freedom to design nimble, evolving, "virtual" teams that could take on various challenges throughout the change journey. This virtual team approach involved assembling teams of volunteers who became committed to, and accountable for, a particular cause. In addition to the aforementioned Executive Innovation Team, as part of a comprehensive plan to engage leaders and employees as change agents, we formed an Extended Innovation Center Team, an

Innovation Communications team, several Innovation Project teams, and a dozen or so teams of Innovation Ambassadors to promote the change program. While it is true that three people cannot change a culture of 6,000 employees, 200 people can, particularly when they begin to feel supported and empowered.

VISIBLE LEADERSHIP

The launch of an innovation program is an opportunity to rewrite the narrative about how the organization functions. It won't happen overnight, but with a persistent emphasis from the leaders of the organization, it will begin to become part of the organization's identity. It's unreasonable for the high-level decision-makers in an organization to expect the culture to change without changing themselves. It's important for the employee base to visibly see the effort these influencers are making to embrace the aspirational value set. The role of demonstrating the culture change cannot be left to a few innovators. After all, the innovators are also expected to be the ones executing the innovation strategy. Organizational leaders must talk about the change process frequently, and more importantly, they must walk the talk. The executive leaders are the ones who tie patterns together for the organization, who create and communicate the vision of the Eiffel Tower, and who lead the way (or get out of the way) so the organization can deliver. The organization is watching. When leaders take risks, and occasionally fail publicly, it sets up an environment where others, who may feel less confident in their ability to experiment, participate in the new culture.

RECOGNIZE, REWARD, AND COMMUNICATE

The importance of recognizing and rewarding the aspirational values when they begin to appear in employee behaviors should go without saying. What is often missed is that the organization should, around the same time, stop rewarding the value set that the organization is moving away from. These types of shifts will take some time to take hold, to become part of the new way of working. It is critical that the shifts are well communicated when they take place so that they are noticed. Employees must understand the new rules of the game to be successful in the new environment; otherwise they will be hesitant to let go of the old trapeze.

CONTROL THE DIRECTION, NOT THE PATH

One of the most challenging aspects of shifting culture occurs when the organization gains its own momentum. The culture program designers, who, no doubt, had their own ideas for how the shift would unfold, will be surprised when the course of change is different than what they'd expected. If they've enlisted others and built an empowering environment for them to lead the way, this is to be expected. The designer must remain dedicated to measuring the shift rather than trying to control every event that occurs, saving energy to course correct when required.

ACCOUNTABILITY

It's easy for a transforming organization to revert to old habits and entrenched norms when the way forward is unclear, or when the organization becomes stressed by outside influences. Patience for nebulous change programs can wear thin when business results are not meeting expectations. Well-designed change programs have mechanisms in place to hold the organization accountable to change. This can take the form of teams of volunteers who both recognize when the organization embodies the aspirational value set, and call the organization out when it fails. Such teams may have skip-level access to executives to share what they're observing in open and honest feedback sessions. For some time, Edmunds.com, a company dedicated to transforming the car buying process, featured an "Authenticity Team," which held the organization accountable to its stated brand values. This team consisted of a few dozen rotating volunteers who listened, measured, and reported on the company's progress to the most senior leaders of the organization.

DESIGN TO REINFORCE, SUSTAIN, AND IMPROVE

While many of the change initiatives, particularly in the change readiness stage, will be temporary pushes that are not necessarily repeatable, it's important to design the aspirational culture to reinforce itself. It's not enough to simply bring a new, aspirational identity into existence if the organization will revert to old habits. The new value set should have sustainability and improvement built into its nature. When the aspirational values begin to appear, it's important to consider what type of motivation or behavioral incentive structure will allow that value to persist, or even better, to improve. Such incentive structures do not necessarily need to involve financial rewards, or even recognition. Often, it's enough to let these values manifest themselves in the new rituals and habits that are being designed. For example, if "continuous improvement" is one of the new, aspirational values, designing retrospective sessions into business processes would reinforce the value by identifying improvement opportunities.

REFLECTION

The best way to truly appreciate any progress that has been made is to stop and reflect, as there will be few milestones or artifacts that you can point to, to say that you're succeeding. For those who are pushing for the change, the job can seem daunting, unending, and thankless. Stopping to appreciate the set of actions and inactions, the moods and emotions, the successes and missteps can recharge their energy for the next push. Further, in order to reinforce the identity, new histories and narratives must be formed. A big part of this new narrative is the remembrance of where the organization has come from, and the recognition of where it is now.

ITERATION

Changing environmental conditions, unexpected and unintended consequences of change efforts, as well as shifts in strategy will all require reexamination of the cultural transformation program. Many successful programs have these iterations built in at a regular cadence, which serves several purposes.

» It allows the teams responsible for designing the change program to follow a predictable, periodic series of steps.

» It allows for the design of decision points that demand executive attention.

» It allows for clear, time-bound expectation setting with those who have enlisted to help the cause. For instance, the Edmunds.com Authenticity Team refreshed its members at the end of each year.

» In the absence of well-defined milestones, a regular cadence allows for the ever-important reflection and celebration of the progress the organization has made.

» Finally, an iterative approach provides natural pivot points with an opportunity to prepare those potentially affected for any upcoming pivots.

Even the most adept change-agents will be surprised by the unforeseeable outcomes of a changing organization. This can be stressful, and these unexpected outcomes can be difficult to contextualize, particularly when in the midst of the change. It might not be until months, or even years, later when the momentous transformation can be recognized or articulated.

During my time at Transamerica, the currents and winds that were continually shifting the course of the business produced a great deal of turbulence. It's only in retrospect that it's clear that the cultural transformation we undertook was successful, putting us in a better position to deal with these winds and. It's challenging to differentiate the change efforts we initiated from the broader set of environmental changes that were taking place. The pressures and stresses felt from low interest rates, expense reduction initiatives, layoffs, reorganizations, and new leadership regimes never ceased. What changed was our ability, as an organization, to talk about the effects of these changes and take action in moving closer to our aspirational identity despite these pressures. We made several high-leverage moves, which helped the organization contextualize and adapt to the new environment. These included rolling out company-wide innovation training, developing a Customer Advocacy Office, advancing our analytics and research capabilities, clamping down on data security vulnerabilities, shutting down highly profitable business lines that had low customer value to reduce reputation risk, revamping the marketing department to be laser-focused on customer experience, and more. These big, structural changes all transformed the business in the right direction, and the agility we displayed in making these changes is nothing short of impressive. However, nothing is absolute, and many of these changes are not still in place today. Strategy and cultural transformation are iterative; the structures and initiatives that were put in place just a few short months ago may no longer be needed today. Often the best you can do is to improve your odds of success amidst the turbulence all around you.

CHAPTER 15: INNOVATION MATURITY STAGES: CULTURAL MATURITY

Unlike organizational strategy, organizational culture will exist whether it's built or not. Top organizations pay more than lip service to building and refining their cultures. A well-designed culture built or rebuilt through a deliberate change program can produce and maintain an empowering innovation environment. Organizations that fail to measure, improve, and iterate their cultures risk misinterpreting the true culture drivers, potentially allowing destructive narratives and values to lurk beneath the surface of what's visible and apparent. Let's revisit the Maturity Stages to further illustrate how organizations in the various stages might differ.

DYSFUNCTIONAL MATURITY STAGE

In Dysfunctional Maturity organizations, the values and structures that exist likely do not support and empower innovation to occur and persist. For example, hierarchical, command-and-control organization structures might stifle creativity and collaboration across departmental lines. Organizations may mistakenly assume that their cultures and real values are well-aligned with the stated values of the organization or its founders. Leaders may socialize effectively only with other leaders, and subscribe to false narratives and be blind to destructive values that disenfranchise and demoralize employees. It may be believed that attention to culture is unimportant, particularly relative to attention to strategy or business results.

TENTATIVE MATURITY STAGE

Organizations who fall into this maturity stage may have stated or aspirational value sets intended to inspire a more nurturing environment for innovation, but they do not fully appreciate or respect the effort required to shift to those values, leaving organizations struggling to realize their true potential. The organization may talk a lot about innovation, but the rewards mechanisms do not match. Innovators may feel conflicted as they fight to innovate in a culture that does not reward or incentivize the value set required to innovate effectively.

CONFIDENT MATURITY STAGE

In Confident Maturity organizations, some work has been done to build an aspirational cultural identity that will allow innovation to flourish. The transformation is underway. In the meantime, these organizations may have compartmentalized innovation or insulated innovation efforts from conflicting value sets, which can so frustrate Today's Innovator. There may be brief periods of innovation mastery, which quickly revert back to more entrenched norms. Executives may underestimate the gravity of the status quo, not appreciating the extent to which legacy narratives and systems continue to anchor the organization to its past.

COMPETENT MASTERY STAGE

Competent masters of innovation have designed a high-functioning innovation environment. Real values that arise which conflict with the aspirational values are quickly addressed and overcome. Innovation-friendly values are not only present, they are sustained and self-reinforced by structures that are expressly designed for that purpose.

CHAPTER 16: RESISTANCE & ROADBLOCKS OF A CULTURE OF INNOVATION

The great management thinker, Peter Drucker, famously declared that "Culture eats strategy for breakfast," recognizing that great strategy is irrelevant if the organizational culture to execute that strategy does not exist. An organization's results will never exceed its current potential, which is a function of talent, resources, strategy, and culture. Too often, organizations ignore or fail to measure the culture variable, frustrating highly talented innovators as they fight to negotiate the roadblocks that the status quo presents. Even with the best resources and clear strategic direction, Today's Innovator will fail to meet expectations when the culture is not supportive and empowering.

A look at common roadblocks or modes of resistance Today's Innovator might encounter while developing and executing a culture change program.

CORE VS. INNOVATION: RESENTMENT

In *Part 1: The Innovation Strategy*, we considered how the organization's core may reject innovation if their respective strategies are misaligned or misunderstood, or competing for common resources. From a cultural perspective, the perceived preference given to innovation initiatives and teams can breed resentment among the core employees. They may feel underappreciated, understaffed, or both, as the new innovation narrative begins to take hold in the organization. This can lead to an unhealthy competitiveness, or worse, uncooperativeness between the core and new factions. While it may be impossible to overcome this dichotomy, organizations should emphasize in their communications the importance and value of the core alongside the emphasis on innovation. Employees in the core may take tremendous pride in the fact that the alternative to not having a strong core is organizational death.

INSUFFICIENT CULTURE CHANGE COMMUNICATIONS

Similar to strategic communications, it is not sufficient to communicate aspirational values in a one-way medium, such as a banner, email, or town hall meeting that is not designed for dialog. Employees should be involved in decisions that matter to them whenever possible. Culture change communications forums must be designed to broadly and repeatedly explore and measure how the change *journey* (not *project*) is interpreted and felt, to provide rationale for change and to answer questions. These forums will introduce the organization to new language, allowing them to hear it in context of storytelling and narratives that they can relate to. Early on in the change journey, organizations must ensure two-way communication forums of inquiry, ideation, feedback, and debate become the norm. Ultimately, organizations should seek to build structures allowing communities of employees to dynamically self-organize and establish sub-cultural identities that reinforce or enhance the aspirational, innovation-friendly values.

NOT WALKING THE TALK

Even when the aspirational identity has been designed and articulated, managers and leaders may fail to appreciate the influence they have rewriting the cultural narratives. While talking about how important it is to transform, they may fail to walk the talk, waiting instead for a few brave employees to take a risk and blaze the trail. This wait can be long. It is the job of a leader to create the environment where employees feel empowered. Empowerment, as we'll cover in some detail in *Part 4: The Profile of Today's Innovator*, is not something simply given to someone. The best way to build empowerment is for managers and leaders to create the space for employees to collaborate, take risks, and be creative. In the absence of a catalyst, these behaviors do not occur on their own. Leaders should help employees build stronger networks, and invite them to participate and engage in the new environment. Further, they should challenge and coach employees through the stages of change, allowing the employees, themselves, to decide upon and build the new structures that will reinforce and sustain the new identity.

ASSUMPTION THAT CULTURE CHANGE IS EASY OR UNIMPORTANT

An empowering environment does not appear naturally. The effort required to not only upset the status quo, but then to build sustaining structures to reinforce a new cultural identity, should not be underestimated. Relative to strategic and financial lessons, very little attention is paid to culture change and organizational psychology in M.B.A. programs, which may cause leaders to assume it is trivial, unimportant, or easy. I'd argue that this occurs because culture change is less objective than what's traditionally taught in business schools; it does not fit the rigidity and prescriptive nature of such instruction. In implementing complex change programs, organizations should not hesitate to enlist the help of external experts and consultants who can coach or lead the transformation program. The perspective of someone who has helped other innovation programs succeed is tremendously valuable. There is no shame in acknowledging that such change requires a mindset and level of empathy that is not commonly found in corporate environments. Organizations wishing to undertake such substantial change efforts may need to make heavy investments in new training, new systems, new communication mechanisms, and new personnel.

KNOWING OVER LEARNING

Culture change requires regular reflection, patterns of learning and ideating to understand what the next, high-leverage opportunity might be. Perhaps the biggest impediment to cultural transformation is decision-makers and influencers who insist they know how to best change the organization. Change patterns are not consistent with "knowing." Even the most self-aware and adept can fall into this trap, believing based on previous experience or training, that they have expert knowledge of how the organization should change. They often insist their ideas are best, and they neither validate their assumptions, nor seek nor respect differing opinions. This can lead to frustration when employees do not feel they have a voice, and can be challenging to overcome, particularly when the "knowers" are in positions of power.

If your organization possesses a "knower" in a position of influence, one effective tactic is to enlist the help of someone this person trusts who is in a position to challenge the assumptions that are being made. Another tactic is continuing to gather and compile data into a convincing case that can be presented to the "knower" at an appropriate later date. If neither of those avenues is reasonable, it may be necessary to ignore, or even undermine that person's authority. If there is no one who is willing to do that, then it might be that the organization simply will not change, until that person is removed from power.

* * *

Today's Innovator must be a leader in inspiring, designing, and promoting change to a continuously improving, innovation-friendly culture. Organizational culture is complex, layered, and sensitive. It is also a powerful force that can spoil any business plan. If a measured, deliberate approach is not taken to designing, redesigning, and continually shifting to some future state identity, cultures can lead to entropy. Complacency, resentment, or even chaos can become pervasive and as Today's Innovator you will encounter terrific cultural forces that present insurmountable resistance to innovation. An environment built to be empowering, nurturing, and sustaining, can be the fuel which drives the innovation competency forward.

PART 3: SYSTEMS OF INNOVATION

"Nobody ever gets credit for fixing problems that never happened."

-Repenning, N. and J. Sterman, MIT
Sloan School of Management

In 2007, I spent six months at a startup, Heritage Union Life Insurance Company, as employee number eleven. I suppose such a gig is a rite of passage to lay claim to the title of "Professional Innovator." The vast majority of the other ten employees, including the founders, were former Capital One employees. Though I hadn't worked with any of them during my eight years at Capital One, I knew what kind of culture I could expect, given the rigor of Capital One's screening for cultural fit.

My eight previous years at Capital One had been a period of incredible growth for me, both personally and professionally, as well as for Capital One. I had matured into a seasoned risk analyst, a product developer, and an innovator. Capital One had morphed in this same period from a nimble, entrepreneurial marketing company, to a process-heavy financial services behemoth concerned with risk management and big, complex projects. Much of my final year at Capital One was spent as a product owner for an Agile team responsible for migrating a several hundred million dollar product onto a new administrative system. The pressure, scope, and rigor of such an undertaking would have been unthinkable in Capital One's early years. This massive system conversion, coupled with intensifying regulatory scrutiny, raised the stress level of the company and left any innovation strategy on the back-burner. It was time to move on.

After a couple months on the new job at the startup, I began to find my groove, developing enough proficiency in life insurance product development and administration to begin to contribute meaningfully to the young company. They trusted me to take on substantial projects, including leading the filing of our company with state Departments of Insurance, conducting deep analysis on early marketing tests, developing a cutting-edge life insurance product, and building a new policy administration system from scratch. The company's strategy was agile, morphing every month. While the culture maintained some resemblance to the Capital One culture I had grown up in, the strategic cadence, decision-making controls, and project execution processes of this tiny company differed substantially from what had been required at the 10,000-plus employee Capital One.

At Capital One, many of the resources you required to innovate were assigned to you from a central project management office. Departments developed annual innovation strategy iterations, and self-funded their own innovation. Technology projects used modified Lean-Agile principles. Decisions were formally approved by a centralized risk management committee. All experimentation required detailed statistical design with rigorous monitoring and reporting plans. These various approaches were designed to work together as a collective *system of innovation* that optimized the resources and streamlined the decisions that thousands of in-flight experiments demand.

Heritage Union innovation was far less orchestrated. Project resources were collected at lunchtime conversations. One budget existed for the entire company. Technology projects were pieced together any way possible. Decisions were made on the fly. Experiments were tracked on whiteboards. This system of innovation was just right for a small company managing a half-dozen in-flight projects, optimizing for speed and scarcity of resources.

The contrast between these two systems of innovation is to be expected, given the circumstances and objectives for each. Anyone selling you a single, guaranteed system of innovation is selling you snake oil. Circumstances change, objectives differ, and the world is just not that predictable. The goal for you as Today's Innovator must be to design and build an innovation system that's right for your company at this point in time. The most effective systems will have built in the competency to iterate and adapt to both the predictable and unpredictable environmental changes to come.

CHAPTER 17: INNOVATION GOVERNANCE

As with *The Innovation Strategy* and the *Culture of Innovation*, shifting the *Systems of Innovation* should follow the same process of assessing the status quo, articulating the future state, developing the roadmap, executing the plan, and iterating. If some of the work on strategy and culture has begun, you should be able to piggyback on that work to inform the approach to shifting the innovation systems.

Anywhere except in the most competent innovative organizations, it is foolish for innovation efforts to follow the same set of rules and requirements that govern all other business-as-usual decisions (yet many organizations will try to force-fit them in). In order to raise the organization's innovation competency, attention must be paid to the design of the decision-making, budgeting, resource assignment, innovation accounting, metrics, and reporting, which comprise the *innovation governance* system.

DECISION-MAKING STRUCTURES

Whether it's bureaucracy, rigid decision rules, ineffective committees, or the endless series of prioritization meetings, there is likely some element of how your organization's core governs its decision-making which has proven to be insufficient for your organization to achieve all of its objectives. Perhaps your organization has been favoring certainty over upside, or rigor over speed, or product improvements over product development. Whatever the limitations are, they must be understood in order to design the decision-making structure which will govern your innovation activity. These shortcomings can be difficult to discern, but the exercise can be made easier by comparing your innovation strategy roadmap to your existing decision-making system, to determine whether the types of outcomes your innovation strategy demands could pass through your decision filters in the time horizon prescribed, without undue burden on the innovators or decision-makers. Similarly, you can also compare your new aspirational value set to the values inherent in your current decision-making structures. There may be some aspirational values related to speed, decisiveness, nimbleness, etc. that are unmet by the structures currently in place.

The factors that must be considered when designing new decision-making structures include: the various types of decisions to be made, who should make what type of decision, the frequency with which decisions should be made, and the various levels of decision authority required (assuming, for instance, that higher risk decisions should require higher levels of authority). If some of your current structures are sufficient, it may be beneficial to leverage as many of them as possible to avoid having to train an entirely new set of behaviors.

Many organizations will choose to embed decision-making directly into the innovation processes they use, eliminating the need for toggling between innovation processes and business-as-usual decision processes. This comes with the added benefit of allowing innovators to make decisions on their own, alleviating the decision-making bottleneck that is all-too-common in today's complex organizations. By developing a set of *screening criteria* that can be used to predetermine whether a new idea, technology, product, or partner is aligned with the innovation strategy, innovators can then make their own decisions inside of an agreed-upon contextual framework. Screening criteria can be classified into categories, such as Strategic Fit, Operational Fit, Brand Fit, Financial Fit, or Consumer Fit. The same screening criteria can be used to evaluate anything from raw ideas, to product concepts, to prototypes, well in advance of a periodic decision-making forum.

Other considerations in the design of decision-making structures include evaluating the different requirements of strategic vs. cultural vs. operational decisions, and determining how frequently the decision-making structures, themselves, will be measured for effectiveness and iterated.

THE INNOVATION BUDGET

Despite what many innovators would like to believe, the money that an organization has available for the purpose of innovating is limited. As I always told my teams, "There is no magic pot of money at our disposal." While there are ways to greatly limit the expense of innovation, it will cost money, and therefore require a budget, to innovate. In Dysfunctional or Tentative maturity organizations, the reality may be that there is no money budgeted for innovation, requiring trade-off decisions to be made. Inside a corporation, this funding might come from shutting down a product or business line that is no longer producing sufficient returns, redirecting money from an existing budget such as Marketing or IT, or expense-reduction initiatives, such as layoffs or cutbacks in operational spending.

Recognizing that there is organizational sacrifice involved in funding innovation, you should err on the side of asking for only as much budget you believe is required to achieve your next objectives. This may require setting your ego aside — there is no sense of managing a large innovation team in a fancy off-site studio office with teams of consultants and freelancers milling about if that is not what the organization requires of innovation. Don't forget the critical question: *What does the organization require from innovation in order to achieve its vision?* If the answer to the critical question is unknown, then so, too, is the answer to the question of *what budget does innovation require from the organization in order to achieve its vision?*

The line items contained in an innovation budget will vary substantially by industry, company size, innovation strategy, and level of innovation maturity. Budgets must have decision-authority assignments to go along with it, as well as periodic budget review and forecasting cycles. Common budget categories include:

» Salary for full-time employees dedicated to innovation

» Salary for part-time or freelance employees

» Consultants and vendors

» Meetings and off-sites

» Travel and conferences

» Training

» Subscriptions and software licenses

» Technology and equipment for research and development

» Real estate for off-site laboratories or co-working spaces

Most innovation programs will find some benefit in hiring consultants, from full-service innovation consultants to independent coaches and speakers. Consultants bring much-needed expertise, experience, and validation to the challenging decisions that innovating organizations will face. Vendors, such as market research companies can provide services at scale that a small innovation team wouldn't otherwise have the resources to develop or afford. Further, businesses may want to consider partnering with other organizations, such as academic programs, accelerators, incubators, or independent laboratories, many of which require funds to enter into. You must recognize, however, that each consultant, vendor, or partner requires some level of active management (including, contracting, periodic calls, site visits, project management, etc.) from someone inside the organization. Don't underestimate this time commitment.

All of the aforementioned spending is fairly straightforward and easy to account for when the innovation strategy is focused on developing new-to-world or new-to-company insights, technologies, products, and capabilities. Some complications arise when innovation efforts overlap with core operations, as may be the case with innovation on existing product lines or enhancements to core business systems. Similarly, it may be unclear which functional group should fund the development of innovation-oriented employee programs, such as training, innovation rooms, or culture-building initiatives. While the innovation program and resources may be the catalyst for such efforts, the cost or benefit may be realized by another business or functional unit. This makes both innovation accounting and innovation project and process resource governance particularly challenging.

PROJECT AND PROCESS RESOURCE GOVERNANCE

One of the primary functions of Today's Innovator is to govern the resources assigned to projects and processes associated with innovation objectives. In an attempt to separate this from the decision of which projects or processes should move forward (which is a strategic development exercise), we'll consider here only the resource allocation exercise. This involves deciding who is assigned, and how much money is invested, in any given effort. Further complicating these resource allocations, as referenced above, is when there is a shared interest with other functions or business units not funded or governed by the innovation budget.

To simplify the resource governance task, you can use an *innovation portfolio* classification scheme to ensure that the level of resource investment across the full set of in-flight innovation initiatives is balanced appropriately relative to the innovation strategy. Portfolio classification is the exercise of assigning innovation initiatives to predefined categories, which can then be prioritized and reported on according to their classifications. Typical categories include:

» A time-horizon dimension, such as *near-term* vs. *medium-term* vs. *long-term*

» A strategic impact dimension, such as *core* vs. *adjacent* vs. *transformational*

» A cost dimension, such as *low*, *medium*, or *high* (as predefined)

» Dimensions related to the strategic vectors identified in the strategy development exercise.

Reviews and reprioritization of the full innovation portfolio can then be conducted at regular intervals corresponding to the organization's strategic or culture change cadences, with an explicit goal of deciding which initiatives will be executed, and by whom, as well as which will not be executed. To prevent any misunderstandings or mistaken expectations, reporting on projects and processes should be robust, making explicit which initiatives are "in flight," as well as what stage of development they are in.

INNOVATION ACCOUNTING

Holding innovation to the same finance and accounting standards as the organization's core can contribute significantly to innovation initiatives failing to gain traction. Innovation carries with it a degree of unmeasurable uncertainty that can make even the most risk-tolerant finance professionals uncomfortable. In the absence of establishing a common understanding and a work-around framework for dealing with innovation's unmeasurables, the organization will look at innovation investments through the same lens as it looks at any investment. For instance, to attain project funding in the core, it may require demonstration that there is a high probability of the investment achieving a standard hurdle rate, or return on investment (ROI). As Today's Innovator, you must work closely with those who will measure and scrutinize innovation investments to develop an innovation accounting system which fits the risk profile of your organization's innovation strategy. For instance, it might be determined in your innovation strategy development exercise that the organization must take significant risks to produce breakthrough innovation in order to reinvent and reestablish itself. This type of moonshot innovation cannot possibly be forecast with year-by-year revenue and ROI projections; that type of forecasting rigor should not be required to fund initiatives classified this way. Adjustments must be made to account for uncertainty, potential upside, and long development time horizons.

Without a doubt, innovation accounting is tricky business. For organizations that are used to managing their finance and accounting in a particular manner, the challenge of measuring the effectiveness of an innovation strategy can be uncomfortable. Further complicating innovation accounting is the line between what is "innovation" and what is "business as usual" is often blurred. Many innovation strategies include objectives focused on the core that require resources from an innovation department or laboratory. This will lead to application of dedicated innovation resources to core projects, or vice versa. Additionally, it will require hand-offs of ideas, concepts, prototypes, products, or even new business lines from the dedicated innovation function back to the core. Such handoffs can be lengthy and iterative, making it near impossible to understand which budget or group should be charged or given credit. What started as a seed of an idea in one part of the organization can end up being a successful program in a completely different area. This can lead to instances where the benefits of innovation are double-counted or represented in multiple sets of financial results and projections.

One of the best ways to overcome these myriad challenges is to enlist the technical experts found in your friendly finance and accounting departments. They will know best how to develop a new system of innovation accounting that will satisfy their requirements, while considering the limitations of what is knowable. This will give finance a meaningful role in what might otherwise be an inaccessible, far-removed, or poorly understood innovation program.

It will likely be the case that different standards of innovation accounting are required for different innovation portfolio classifications. Developing various *financial scorecards* to measure the costs and benefits of innovation by category can help measure the degree to which the innovation efforts are satisfying what is expected of them. Innovation that focuses on core operations will likely be more predictable, and therefore included in financial forecasts. Innovation that is far out on the time horizon, or far removed from the core, will be far less predictable, and the decision may be made not to include these initiatives in revenue projections, the scorecard instead focusing on measuring costs, early returns, or developing market estimates.

As we introduced in *Part 1: The Innovation Strategy*, the *ultimate scorecard* for innovation should be whether the organization, as a whole, is on-track to achieve its objectives. After all, if the status quo were working, innovation wouldn't be needed. Viewed in this light, it becomes less critical to make sense of the blurred line between innovation and the core. However, for you as Today's Innovator, the idea of being on the hook for the organization, as a whole, to get back on track may feel unfair or unattainable. This is precisely why it is so critical for you to be intimately involved in the development and articulation of the innovation strategy. If the resources and costs that the organization is willing or able to put towards the innovation strategy are not sufficient to execute the strategy, that is something that must be addressed before the innovators are turned loose.

METRICS AND REPORTING

An important aspect of both project and process resource governance and innovation accounting is the establishment of regular reporting or dashboarding to stakeholders on initiatives associated with the innovation strategy. The most effective reports are concise, consistent, and categorized, showing metrics of interest and the status of any in-flight initiatives. The best reports go beyond consideration of just the in-flight initiatives to present the work which remains to be done, or which is *not* happening, the whole of which is called the organization's *innovation pipeline*. Further, the best reports present an organization-wide view, including initiatives that are executed by resources outside of the control of the report owner; and they demonstrate how this work is helping the organization achieve its vision, repeatedly justifying investment in innovation as an organization-wide competency.

Many organizations stuck in their status quo will expect innovation reporting and dashboarding to contain a standard battery of financial metrics, such as costs, revenue projections, net present value, etc. While some of these are useful for directional purposes, such as to demonstrate the potential of the initiative, they can be wildly inaccurate. Tying any such projection to a project with a high degree of uncertainty can anchor decision-makers to the projections. Instead, it is useful to agree upon a set of *metrics that matter* for innovation initiatives which might vary by portfolio classification. Such a portfolio classification approach to reporting can account for the varying level of detail available within each category as well as differences in the importance or interest level of the stakeholders by category. For instance, for that moonshot-type initiative that we considered in Innovation Accounting above, maybe the most important metrics are *input metrics* such as how many full-time employees are involved, how many experts have been interviewed, how many ideas are under serious consideration, or how big the marketplace opportunity might be. Input metrics can be valuable leading indicators, which point to the potential of a given initiative without requiring the innovators to forecast a financial outcome in the absence of reliably predictive data.

CHAPTER 18: THE INNOVATION ECOSYSTEM

As mentioned previously, the development of the overall innovation governance system requires the same iterative approach as both strategy development and cultural program development. It is not the case that all of these governance activities can be flipped "on" like a switch and suddenly you have an effective system. It requires continuous improvement with each iteration. The same is true of the development of the *Innovation Ecosystem.*

Whereas, a well-developed *innovation governance* system can ensure that the activity related to innovation is well-considered and well-understood, it is the design of a highly effective *innovation ecosystem* which can improve its quality and impact.

The innovation ecosystem can be defined as the way in which, and the environment in which, innovation is executed. Similar to culture, the innovation ecosystem exists whether it is designed or not — innovators and leaders will find a way to get their jobs done. Of course, as with culture, the most effective systems are intentional, not left to chance. At a minimum, the ecosystem consists of the resources that are in any way involved in innovation activity (the stakeholders), the way the resources are organized, the physical environment in which innovation takes place, the methods and processes which are employed, the technical or mechanical systems on which innovation will occur, and the rewards system. There will likely be additional characteristics of the ecosystem, which should be measured and designed specific to your situation. For this reason, perhaps the most important factor in the design and implementation of a highly effective innovation ecosystem is to what degree you understand what is working well, and what is not.

CURRENT STATE ANALYSIS AND FUTURE STATE DESIGN

Empathy is required of Today's Innovator to understand the effectiveness of your current state innovation ecosystem. You must strive to learn the actions, inactions, needs, preferences, and motivations of those who innovate in the current environment. Your empathy muscle will be tested as the tendency to judge the elements of the ecosystem for anything, but their effectiveness can lead to inefficient design of a new system (or a design that is incorrect given the current conditions and innovation requirements of the organization). An example of this might be to favor the use of a specific innovation process because there is a best-selling book popularizing it, instead of objectively observing and measuring its potential relative to the current state. Fortunately, it is the very same empathy muscle that innovators traditionally train to identify consumer needs and pain points that will yield insight as to what are the most intense needs and pain points of the innovation ecosystem.

Both interviews (discussion) and ethnographies (observation) are effective tools for empathetically assessing the current state of innovation. Organizational leaders and internal innovators (a.k.a. *intrapreneurs)* will tell wonderful stories of what it takes to accomplish innovation inside of the organization. They will expose all the tricks, influencers, back-channels, shortcuts, hurdles, redundancies, and more. Patterns emerge from those stories that should be considered as data points in the design of the future state. Again, you must be careful not to dismiss the importance of one of these data points by placing your own judgment on its value. As another example, it might be the case that there is a powerful gatekeeper that everyone must win over in order to get a project or initiative executed. It is important then to consider why that person's opinion carries so much significance and whether it is something that will persist when designing the future state ecosystem. To dismiss their opinion as not important to the innovation strategy may prove to be a costly blunder when the gatekeeper wields their power to slow down or halt innovation execution down the line.

Once you've got your current state ecosystem sufficiently mapped out, the exercise of designing the future state begins. Be sure to align this design with the innovation strategy and future state identity/aspirational values you've identified for your team or organization. If rapid prototyping is important, or if incorporating innovation into your brand is important, you'll likely design a different ecosystem than if you're building new technology platforms, or if you plan to partner with accelerators. Then, build your roadmap to determine who will be developing which elements of the ecosystem, who will govern the decisions related to ecosystem development, what your cadence is for revisiting the current state and design, etc.

Finally, execute the first set of initiatives and any corresponding training or orientation sessions, and iterate to continuously improve. When revisiting the current state assessment during each iteration, make sure you've measured the changes to the ecosystem with a goal of identifying and sharing best practices to help other innovators overcome any barriers they may encounter.

Many design considerations of an effective innovation ecosystem are summarized below. It's necessary to restate here that if you're reading this book hoping to learn the perfect system of innovation, this consideration set will disappoint you. This is not a prescription as to how to set up your organization. Rather, its intent is to help you design a better innovation ecosystem for your organization at this point in time.

STAKEHOLDER IDENTIFICATION & ALIGNMENT

An easy place to begin in the assessment and design of your innovation ecosystem is to identify the stakeholders and the roles they will play in the innovation program.

Your organization's set of internal innovation stakeholders may include the management board and other decision-makers. Also, it may include dedicated innovators, users of innovation capabilities, and shared execution resources. Further, consider experts, specialized resources, employees who must be apprised of progress, business units, and functional groups, among your innovation stakeholders. Building a comprehensive list of the stakeholders will help you in the design of the rest of the elements, most notably the organizational chart, and the selection of appropriate methods and processes for your program.

An important element of the innovation ecosystem roadmap is to build in orientation or training sessions for each of the new elements that are developed. Be sure to make these sessions available to as many of the stakeholders as possible to initiate the process of institutionalization of the elements. Even a seemingly far-removed stakeholder, such as a regional sales director, would benefit, for instance, if they are touting the organization's cutting-edge innovation processes in their sales presentations.

You may wish to design a role specifically for the broader set of employees in your organization to keep them aware, engaged, and involved in your innovation program. This could include development of *experience rooms* designed to familiarize employees with your customers or technologies, as well as methods for gathering ideas from the employee community.

The external stakeholder set may include consultants, vendors, business partners, and much more. Staying on top of the external stakeholder landscape will require considerable energy. As Today's Innovator, you owe it to the organization to evaluate the value that external parties might add, even if it means carving out large chunks of your time for sales pitches and product demos. Emerging startups could become partnership, acquisition, or joint venture targets. Accelerators, incubators, universities, and outside labs can expose your organization to positive public relations, new insights, creative solutions, or cutting-edge advances in technology or science. Conferences, trade organizations, and association memberships can provide unique insight into marketplace problems, help to identify new methodologies, or make connections to potential partners.

Once the future state stakeholders are identified, your roadmap should include an alignment plan to ensure that it's clear how this ecosphere of stakeholders will interact within the innovation ecosystem. This may help you identify new communication mechanisms. It may also expose the need for teambuilding or alignment sessions. And finally, it may help you understand which stakeholders seem to be "on board" with the innovation program and which might offer some resistance to change.

ORGANIZING AND HIRING FOR INNOVATION

Many of Today's Innovators aren't afforded the luxury of influencing the initial organizational scheme for their innovation program. Some are simply leaders who have been asked to innovate in their departments, others were hand-selected to be on an innovation team, and others are splitting time between innovation and their regular duties. This is particularly true of Dysfunctional and Tentative Maturity organizations which might still be experimenting with innovation. With the knowledge you'll gain of what's working (and not working) in your innovation ecosystem, don't underestimate the influence that your voice has in determining future iterations of the organizational.

As with all of these ecosystem elements, it's important to turn back to the critical question, *"What does the organization require of innovation to achieve its vision?"* in order to inform the design of the optimal organizational scheme. Similarly, as with all of these elements, there is no *right* way to organize or hire for innovation. The best organizational scheme today may not be your best organizational scheme tomorrow. Consider, again, what are the aspirational values for the innovation program? For instance, if nimbleness, agility, and responsiveness are among those values, you may consider a very fluid, or flat, organizational scheme.

Decisions such as the appointment of a Chief Innovation Officer (CInO) or Head of Innovation, can feel fairly permanent, so companies and organizations tend to be cautious in their approach to hiring into such roles. For example, a business leader or a small team of business leaders may initially be identified to lead innovation, which will eventually lead to a longer-term organizational design. If it is your aspiration to become a CInO, your best bet may be to establish yourself as an innovation leader within an organization, then build the case for the organization to hire you as the CInO.

Some organizations may choose to tout "innovation everywhere" with the expectation that all employees develop and display the innovation competency. Others may identify a dedicated innovation team or department comprised of high-performing employees from within the business. The role of dedicated teams may be to facilitate innovation activities, or to be the innovators, or both. Still other organizations may select employees to participate in innovation teams temporarily, and then rotate back into their prior roles.

Another common organizational model is to create functional centers of excellence, which make available a particular capability, such as digital development or market research, as a centralized resource to support innovation efforts across the organizations. Don't be surprised if these functions are initially centralized, then decentralized, then centralized again, and so on, in a cycle which adapts to changing organizational needs.

Once the initial organizational scheme is established, be sure to measure the new cultural narratives, or any unintended consequences, that it creates. For instance, if an innovation department organizational chart is built as a hierarchy with an innovation leader at the top, a handful of mid-level managers, and a few dozen lower-level employees, then you may find that command-and-control values typical of a hierarchy will naturally appear. If you're structured that way, but expect employees to self-organize into innovation teams without their manager's input, you may find a reluctance to act without permission.

Additional considerations with respect to organizational design include defining the role of people managers, and how to assign roles and responsibilities in the chosen organizational scheme. An important distinction to make is that organizational charts do not, themselves, define the way that a team, department, or organization works. They are not the same as how a team, department, or organization operates. A product owner or virtual team leader may have far more influence on an employee's duties and development than the employee's direct manager. The expected roles, responsibilities, and interaction models should be made clear.

Many organizations will launch their innovation programs with a small set of high-performing current employees, then plan to add new skill sets and experience through hiring and staffing strategies. You must exercise some care hiring innovators from outside an established organization. External hires into innovation roles will likely be valued for thinking differently, which, as we covered in *Part 2: Culture of Innovation*, will be the very reason that they will meet resistance. They must either be resilient enough to weather the rough patches of resistance, or insulated enough from the core business to not rub up against the status quo. All that said, it is incredibly important to find ways to inject new thinking into your innovation program. Some common strategies include: hiring from smaller organizations who can bring experience with rapid iteration, hiring for broad experience (such as from management consultants), or hiring an entrepreneur-in-residence (EIR) to build an expansive innovation strategy alongside the CEO. Some organizations will choose to remain lean and rely, instead, on consultants, contractors, temporary staff, or freelancers, to meet the ever-changing talent demands of an innovation portfolio. Hiring freelancers, or staff-on-demand, can provide an advantage in flexibility that's not possible with full-time staff. A lean team can leverage a strong network of volunteers, quasi-dedicated employees, and rotating employees to inject fresh perspective and specific expertise when needed. Additionally, this approach will reduce overhead while exposing more people in the organization to innovation activity.

PHYSICAL ENVIRONMENT

The right organizational scheme for your organization may be a function of how you design your physical innovation environment, which is likely a function of what your innovation strategy is. The primary choice is whether to build an internal innovation space or an external innovation lab. Each can be highly customizable to suit your organization's needs. I'll use the terms *lab* and *space* rather interchangeably, recognizing that use of the term *lab* may imply an added level of focus or dedication.

The external innovation lab exists in a separate building either near the main site, or well off-site, sometimes located in a separate city from the main operations. Often these remote spaces are focused on a specific innovation type requiring specialized equipment, technology, or focus, such as a "Test Kitchen" or "Data Innovation Lab." They generally require a team or department of dedicated resources that are fairly independent from the core, and are sometimes part of a different sub-company all together.

If there is an expectation of frequent, efficient communications between the innovation program and the core, an internal innovation lab would be a better option. An internal innovation lab might describe a room or a partitioned area within a company's building that is dedicated to innovation. Similar in function to external labs, these spaces can be useful for either dedicated, independent innovation teams or for cross-functional teams who cycle through the lab on a project basis. Elements of both internal and external labs may include reception areas, team workspaces, huddle rooms, lounge areas, presentation spaces, customer observation rooms, kitchens, and game areas.

Organizations who are trying to integrate innovation as a strategic thread through all of their activities, or who are trying to create an innovative culture, may choose to transform their office spaces into more inviting, collaborative innovation environments. Office cubicle walls might be lowered to promote more collaboration. Investments might be made in fancy java bars, or "collision spaces," which force employees to interact in certain locations and, of course, banners might be hung promoting the new, aspirational values!)

The most important consideration for the physical environment is to have specific goals and values in mind when designing it, and to understand how it will operate. But while the space may help with collaboration or creativity, know that it will not execute your innovation strategy for you, so be sure to be budget-conscious. In fact, it may be hard to believe, but innovation can be accomplished without any investment in a new physical environment! While there may be good reasons to build fancy, off-site innovation labs, such as Progressive Insurance's *Innovation Garage,* you'll probably be able to get similar results with a dedicated room inside your building (at least initially). As with anything, a test-and-learn approach can allow for "fast failure" before scaling.

INNOVATION METHODS AND PROCESSES

If the physical environment is the skeleton of the innovation ecosystem, the chosen innovation methods and processes are its circulatory system. They will govern how information and decisions move through the innovation lifecycle, from idea to launch.

Many organizations starting out on their innovation journey may send a few employees to innovation training, or invite a consultant in to facilitate a workshop. A training workshop can be a nice starting point to stimulate discussion and interest, but this type of experience may do little to install a repeatable, effective, end-to-end system of innovation.

The selection of the right set of methods and processes for your organization depends in large part on how you've decided to structure the physical environment, as well as what the innovation strategy is. It may be the case that the selections will be used only by the innovators, whereas in other instances a complete change to the entire organization's processes may be in order.

But the closest-held secret of innovation processes is this: Effectively, all innovation processes are all the same. If you put two people in separate rooms and ask them to design an end-to-end innovation process, after some time they will both, for the most part, come out and describe the same sequence. Innovators should start with insight or a business problem, then creatively identify solutions to the problem, then select viable solutions to test, then conceptualize or prototype the top ideas, then analyze the effectiveness of the concept/prototype to solve the problem, then iterate as needed, then scale up.

This basic process is exhaustively detailed in books, packaged as fancy flow charts, trademarked and branded by consultants, and endlessly debated at innovation conferences. But, the truth is that learning and managing innovation processes doesn't need to be a burden. A bare-bones process can be sufficient to move the organization from where it is to where it needs to be.

Here, we'll touch upon some of the most popular methods and processes that successful organizations use either as variations on the basic process, or as additional methods to complement the basic process. This is by no means an exhaustive list:

>> Comprehensive processes:

>> The *stage-gate process* is the tried and tested standard for installing innovation discipline and rigor, ensuring leaders maintain

control over decision-making at predefined decision *gates*. These are particularly common when the innovators are working in or on the core, which requires a certain level of control or predictability.

» *Lean Startup* is a process first made popular in startups but found to be particularly effective inside complex organizations that wish to innovate outside of their core operations. It stresses building only *minimally viable products* (MVPs) at first, and moving forward in small, rapid iterations.

» *Design Thinking* is a philosophy, more than a process, which places customer empathy and idea generation at the core of the solution process. Popularized at Stanford, there are now many variations of Design Thinking found in universities and corporations around the world.

» Similarly, *human-centric design* is a philosophy which focuses on humans through the design process. It applies ergonomics and/or usability principles to design product features preferred by humans.

» *Hackathons* can be designed to allow small, cross-functional teams to build solutions to specific business problems in very short spurts, often held over 48 hours. Solutions usually are taken all the way to prototype stage, so the organization can test the top solutions immediately after the Hackathon.

» *Front-End* Research and Ideation methods:

  » *Focus groups* and *surveys* are traditional market research techniques that actively seek customer perspective.

  » *Ethnographies* or simply "getting out of the building" are effective for observing customer or human behavior.

  » For organizations who don't have enough time, resources, or interest in conducting their own research, *white papers* and *syndicated research* sources can provide insight sometimes as rich as those mentioned above.

» *Persona* development, *customer journey mapping*, and *empathy mapping* have recently gained popularity, particularly in Design Thinking and customer experience design processes.

» *Brainstorming* sessions are the traditional approach to ideation, consisting of round tables, easels, post-it notes, bowls of Skittles, and a handful of Rubik's Cubes and Legos thrown in a pile on the tables. Training and preparation of the facilitator can make all the difference between a brainstorming session being highly effective, or a waste of time.

» *Six Thinking Hats* is a series of techniques designed so that ideators represent different viewpoints, in order to uncover creative solutions.

» *Storyboarding, idea webs,* and *SCAMPER* are examples of popular techniques used in brainstorming/ideation that can be combined with other techniques to spur creativity.

» Various *idea management* software solutions exist to assist with the collection, storing, sorting, scoring, and voting on ideas. Many of these have "suggestion box" capabilities which allow for ongoing idea collection.

» *Back-End* Development and Process Management methods:

» Originally dreamed up as a manifesto for improving software development, *Agile* is an effective philosophy for taking dedicated teams through short sprints of work, promoting team commitment, customer intimacy, independence, and creativity. Agile is most effective when timelines and resources are fixed, but the scope of a project is unknown or negotiable.

» *Scrum* is an Agile variation which scales the simplest, most repeatable aspects of Agile to be used in more complex projects.

» *Waterfall* development is the traditional process of executing a robust, often complex, business plan according to predefined specifications (as opposed to Agile where the specifications can change iteratively). Waterfall uses project managers and process managers, and is typically used when the scope and timeline of a project are fixed. Waterfall can be useful when developing or implementing new technology systems on which innovation will occur.

» Traditional *business process management* (BPM) tools can be effective in innovation teams, particularly Gantt charts to describe phases, swimlanes to describe roles and responsibilities within a process, and RACI or RASCI matrices (Responsible, Accountable, Supporting, Consulted, Informed) to assign specific roles and interaction models to resources within a project.

» Finally, there is nothing preventing innovators from developing the technical expertise to prototype and develop for themselves. Consider the benefits of expanding skill sets into coding, creative design, digital development, engineering, machining, cooking, chemistry, or whatever your innovation strategy requires. The more expertise each innovator can bring to a team, the faster and more proficient the team will become.

While most of these methods are straightforward, training can be found for each to achieve higher degrees of proficiency. In the interest of continuously improving, Today's Innovator should spend a not-insignificant fraction of time on training, and these methods and processes are great places to start. However, be careful of believing that any of these methods are the *only* or even *best* way to innovate — a common dogma that is promoted by practitioners dedicated to preserving and perfecting these approaches. While many of them have, indeed, improved upon innovation best practices and eliminated process waste, rest assured that the next process "savior" is lying in wait, ready to be released at a conference or bookstore near you, and primed to inspire a mania that gives rise to new associations and university programs.

TECHNOLOGICAL READINESS

Perhaps the most under-appreciated, yet potentially paralyzing, element of the innovation ecosystem is an organization's technological readiness to innovate. Innovators and leaders can become entranced and enamored by flashy consultant workshops focusing on creativity and idea collection. But the best idea in the world can never go to market if the technology, machine, or *platform* required to produce it does not exist, or if there are development bottlenecks typically found in resource-constrained technology organizations. Many innovation programs lose steam when the exciting concepts they've dreamed up take months, or even years, to build. This degrades confidence in innovation and presents the risk of allowing a competitor to jump through a small window of opportunity first.

As part of the current state ecosystem analysis, innovators should identify the business systems, technology platforms, or machines that are ready for innovation to occur. In many organizations, these business systems, technology platforms, or machines simply do not exist — or at least do not have the capacity or flexibility to produce what the innovation strategy demands. If this is the case in your organization, it must be treated with priority to develop them. It provides a wonderful opportunity for the innovation resources to align themselves with the IT or engineering groups to design and implement a technological readiness strategy.

What might be uncovered during the current state ecosystem analysis is that there is either a rigid technological architecture, which lacks the ability to customize quickly, or maybe a complex, disjointed architecture which requires rigorous integration testing to ensure that solutions don't produce unintended consequences. Ideally, the future state ecosystem should contain systems, technological platforms, or machines that allow for innovators to rapidly prototype and test without the threat of impacting the production systems. These can take many forms:

» Strategic application program interface (API) frameworks can be designed specifically for innovation.

» Virtual environments (VE), sandboxes, or test environments allow for prototype development in non-production environments.

» Middleware solutions can link rigid enterprise systems to platforms or localized systems on which innovation can occur.

» User-friendly systems such as content management systems (CMS) allow for non-technical resources to conduct otherwise technical testing.

» Business intelligence (BI) or non-production data repositories can be accessed for data modeling or analytical purposes.

If innovation resources are idly waiting for these innovation-ready systems to come online, they can spend time generating quick wins where a suitable innovation-ready environment already exists (or where such a platform is not required at all, such as developing new marketing messages).

REWARDS

The final innovation ecosystem consideration that we'll cover is that of *rewards*. It is human nature to be motivated by rewards structures, whether those rewards are incentives designed specifically to motivate a particular behavior, or whether a particular behavior is reinforced by an organization's culture. Regardless, it feels good to be recognized, and when that happens, you'll be motivated to continue that behavior.

Innovation rewards structures come in all shapes and sizes, from small, goofy, team recognition efforts, such as giving a chosen team member a coveted trophy or token to proudly display, to large, formal, organization-wide or industry-wide awards, such as an annual monetary award shared by the "most innovative team" in an organization. The effectiveness of either of these approaches is up for debate, particularly when the employees are simply doing what the culture expects of them (doing their job), but there is certainly no harm. At the very least these rituals can become predictable patterns that enter into cultural narratives.

As Today's Innovator, what you should aspire to is developing self-sustaining, cultural rewards mechanisms which are persistent and values-based. For instance, if it is embedded in your cultural value set to invite collaborators from all corners of the organization to help solve complex business problems, then this becomes a behavior that no longer requires explicit incentives. The motivation for collaboration comes from the empowerment built by having seen others behave that way, knowing others expect you to behave that way, and having a common language and mechanisms for inviting such collaboration. Of course, like everything else we've covered, there is no "on" switch to flip that can activate such an intrinsic rewards system. But one thing is for sure: a positive, motivating, intrinsic rewards system is unlikely to arise by itself. It must be set as an objective, designed, implemented, measured, and iterated to get to that place.

CHAPTER 19: ROLE OF TODAY'S INNOVATOR: SYSTEMS OF INNOVATION

It is the job of Today's Innovator to identify the best approaches to innovation governance in establishing the innovation ecosystem. This is a daunting task, but it most certainly can be phased to make it manageable. Further, if you've got an innovation strategy roadmap and a regular cadence for innovation strategy iterations, the roadmap for improving the systems of innovation can be integrated into that. Then, it becomes a matter of expanding your current state strategy assessment and strategic objective setting exercises to include systems of innovation in their scope.

Once you are settled into a regular cycle of improving upon these elements, your attention can turn to building and maintaining a record of the complete governance system and ecosystem so that others can be readily oriented to the systems of innovation inside your organization. It may be wise to partner with Human Resources or a Talent Development resource to implement and regularly update training or orientation sessions related to the innovation competency. For instance, if any of the innovation resources are earmarked to support the core, then it is important for the employees within the core to understand how they can utilize these resources.

CHAPTER 20: INNOVATION MATURITY STAGES: SYSTEMS OF INNOVATION

There are many decisions to make in the design of effective systems of innovation. It's unlikely that either the organization's status quo or its first attempt at designing the innovation governance system and ecosystem would be effective enough to satisfy the innovators and the innovation stakeholders. As Today's Innovator you must be willing to experiment with and iterate these systems. As an organization's innovation maturity progresses, these systems will become more robust and should become easier to tweak or adjust. Let's revisit the Maturity Stages to illustrate how organizations in the various stages might differ.

DYSFUNCTIONAL MATURITY STAGE

Dysfunctional Maturity organizations are likely attempting to use their core decision-making, accounting, and reporting structures to make investment decisions in their innovation program. Leaders of departments or business units are likely the ones being asked to lead innovation with a miniscule budget and limited dedicated resources. Until the program gains confidence and commitment, these organizations are not making big decisions, such as reorganizing for innovation, hiring new innovators, or modifying the physical environment.

TENTATIVE MATURITY STAGE

In the Tentative Maturity stage, organizations have recognized the limitations of the core for governing innovation and have begun to make adjustments. Consultants, vendors, or innovation partners may have been identified, and the excitement is growing. The organization may have carved out full-time, dedicated innovation resources, likely utilizing high-performing talent from existing business lines. A small team or two may be exploring new ideas, perhaps fully occupying a conference room in the building, or experimenting with working from a near-site external workspace. Few ideas are advancing past the ideation stage. Some rewards mechanisms for innovation have been identified, but they are not consistently understood.

CONFIDENT MATURITY STAGE

Organizations in this stage have developed new innovation governance structures, such as a dedicated budget, new reporting, and maybe identified a committee for making innovation decisions with less bureaucratic overhead than is found in the core. Confident organizations have likely appointed an innovation leader, such as a Chief Innovation Officer or Head of Innovation. Innovation teams are well-formed and no longer rely on poaching top talent from the core business lines. Some widespread physical space transformation may have occurred, making innovation spaces available for all employees, and an external lab may have launched. Several innovation objectives have been met, with some in-market successes, but these have likely caused conflict in competition for core resources.

COMPETENT MASTERY STAGE

The governance structures of innovation activity have become indiscernible from core governance structures. Innovation-related roles likely have disappeared entirely, as innovation-friendly values and the innovation job function is now fully absorbed into all job descriptions and expectations. Some longer-term, business-critical, or exploratory focus areas are firmly established in onsite or offsite laboratories, perhaps using their own brand or co-brand. All lines of business are innovating consistently, and very few resources are utilized explicitly for maintaining the core.

CHAPTER 21: RESISTANCE & ROADBLOCKS OF SYSTEMS OF INNOVATION

A look at common roadblocks or modes of resistance Today's Innovator might encounter while developing and implementing new systems of innovation:

UNINTENDED CONSEQUENCES

There is no doubt that the benefits of a well-designed system of innovation and an innovation-friendly culture can be significant. Shareholders can anticipate business growth, customers can take advantage of expanded product and feature offerings, and employees can feel a stronger sense of empowerment, purpose, and inclusion as they aspire and unite to take the organization to greater heights. The culture can become dynamic, rallying around complex business problems to continuously improve itself with very little direction from above. Innovators may find that progress and wins come quicker and more consistently as more adjustments are made to the systems of innovation. However, each of these new traits can give rise to unintended consequences that, if left unchecked, can prevent the organization from realizing its new level of potential. For instance, a new innovation rewards program can be divisive or viewed as elitist if core resources who are bogged down by day-to-day issues don't feel they have a fair chance at attaining the rewards. As Today's Innovator, you must be sure to measure the way in which culture change programs and systems of innovation changes are received to ensure that they are producing their intended effects.

EGO

For many leaders, the primary intrinsic reward that reinforces their behavior is the confidence they gain when their ego is boosted. Unfortunately, leadership ego can get in the way of effective teamwork, reinforcing silos and creating unhealthy competition. To receive their confidence boost, leaders might seek credit (both personal credit, or to include in their businesses reporting) for innovation initiatives that are gaining traction. Ego may lead them to compete with their peers for innovation resources that can improve their own business lines, often not considering what is best for the organization as a whole. They may even vie for complete control of innovation resources and their initiatives. Ego will affect innovation leaders as well, who may seek to acquire and control more resources (people and dollars) than is required to execute the innovation strategy. This will only make their job more complex and may raise the expectations of what they can accomplish to unreasonably high levels. Today's Innovator needs to be acutely aware of these implications on their activities and design the systems of innovation to mitigate the effects of ego. For instance, designing irrefutable innovation accounting and decision rules, governing the innovation budget closely, or developing reporting that makes clear which business lines should gain credit for in-flight initiatives might keep egos in check and give appropriate credit where credit is due.

TOO MUCH, TOO SOON

Organizations which rush into innovation, hoping for outcomes before the competency is built, might expect too much from innovation before it is reasonable to believe it could succeed. In the absence of a well-designed innovation ecosystem, innovators may get stuck in the "front-end" of innovation, spending a majority of their time in search or discovery phases. Without technological readiness, or strong alignment with expert or specialized resources, there may be nowhere for these front-end ideas and concepts to be developed.

FUNCTIONAL GROUP MISALIGNMENT

At one of my previous employers, innovation was declared a priority and celebrated as a new cultural value that would allow us to accelerate our growth. Immediately after this declaration, the business decided upon who the innovators would be, and even set aside a sizeable budget. The innovators were then set loose to innovate. We failed to put the necessary structural changes in place for innovation to take hold. By simply bolting it on to the existing structure of the business, and treating innovation as a department, rather than a competency, the innovators met unnecessary resistance with every other functional group they encountered. For example, Human Resources wasn't prepared to adjust its staffing practices to meet the speed and specialization that innovation demanded; the Legal Department became unsettled by risk that the innovators were introducing into the business; the Finance Department demanded detailed financial forecasts from the innovators from new product lines that didn't yet exist; and the core business lines were not prepared to commercialize the prototypes that the innovators developed. It is decidedly your role as Today's Innovator to anticipate the challenges of aligning with organizational resources and to develop a plan for overcoming these challenges. It is unreasonable to assume that these functional groups will change themselves to become a high-functioning, innovative organization. It is up to you to establish clear roles, responsibilities, and expectations with each of these functional groups, and to continue to iterate and improve over time. Innovation must be demystified for these groups, and they should have open access to the progress updates, reporting, and communications that relate to them.

COMPLEX HANDOFFS

Systems of Innovation inside complex organizations must allow for products or features to pass through development stages rather seamlessly. The transition processes must be designed to limit the loss of accountability, customer need information, decision history, or technical specifications that might occur when an innovation is handed off to a core business line or technical team. Additionally, there must be a commonly understood language to make clear which stage something is in, and what exactly that means. Some organizations will use terms like *conceptualization, prototyping, alpha testing,* and *beta testing* as stage labels, each of which would have a clear definition. Innovation accounting rules can then be assigned to the various stages to determine which business unit is funding or recognizing the revenue of the innovation. Organizations may wish to assign a *product owner* to each innovation to act as the key stakeholder who will remain accountable for products throughout the lifecycle, regardless of handoffs. Alternatively, organizations can attempt to innovate entirely without handoffs, allowing teams to see their projects through from idea to launch, and beyond. This is frequently found in long-time horizon projects that are far removed from the organization's core.

* * *

At this point, it's likely you're feeling a bit overwhelmed by all of the program design factors Today's Innovator must consider. Perhaps you're wondering if it is too much to ask of an innovator, to design the innovation strategy, change the culture, and build the systems of innovation required to achieve your organization's objectives. Truth be told, it *is* too much to ask of an innovator, but it is not too much to ask of an innovation *community*. Whether your community takes the form of a formal innovation team or if it's just a set of employees volunteering to help the innovation cause, rest assured that there are others who want to help. In the final part, *A Portrait of Today's Innovator*, we will discuss what a successful innovator in today's fast-paced world looks like, both as an *innovation leader*, and as an *individual*.

PART 4: A PORTRAIT OF TODAY'S INNOVATOR

The sea is rarely calm for long. The navigator knows that a strong wind is coming, and must be prepared for it to come from any direction.

It wasn't until high school that I began to enjoy mathematics. Before then, I had been successful with my math classes, but I didn't take an interest in it. It was too much about rote memorization and ritual, constantly reenacting the same steps that millions of students had taken before me. My ninth grade math teacher, Mrs. Steiper, changed that perspective for me.

Mrs. Steiper knew me as a "B" student. I didn't take notes. I took no care with my homework. I rushed through my tests, making silly errors. After one such test, I was beaming from having finished it in record time. Mrs. Steiper walked slowly towards my desk, being careful not to disturb my peers around me. She laid a paper on my desk, then circled around back to the front of the room.

Glancing down at the paper, I was surprised to see that it contained a mathematical puzzle of sorts. I picked up my pencil and began to work on the challenging puzzle, which consisted of different paths I could explore. Not knowing which to take, I tested several of the paths before finally choosing a tact and sticking to it. Before I knew it, the math class was over. All the other students had turned in their tests and left the room. Mrs. Steiper made her way over to me.

"Did you figure it out?" she might have said.

"Kind of," I may have replied. "I tried a few things that didn't work, but then realized that…" I went on to explain my logic, showing her my result at the end. She nodded her head in approval and then pointed out that I was running late to my next class.

This pattern repeated itself throughout the school year. Ironically, it gave me more incentive to rush through my tests, knowing that Mrs. Steiper would provide me with something more interesting to pass the time. Late in the school year, I finally had a chance to sit down with her and talk about these puzzles. In that conversation is when I internalized for the first time that I might be good at math. She encouraged me, telling me I had a strength, and to stick to it. I remember sharing with her that

I didn't really enjoy the math we were working on in class — I didn't like memorizing formulas, or producing "text book" answers in which I showed my work, when I knew I could skip steps and simply show the result.

"All those puzzles I gave to you, did you enjoy them?"

"Of course!"

"Those are all math problems that require formulas to solve," she said. "The thing is, you solved them without memorizing a formula."

I must have disagreed with her; I believed my solutions to be more creative than formulaic. She had me pull some of them out and we went through them together. In each instance, she was able to find a step I had taken that she circled in her trademark red ink.

"These are the formulas here," she said, pointing to what she'd circled. "You didn't have these memorized. You were able to derive and discover them on your own. But, of course, you do have to know your fundamentals to find them. There are other formulas you could have derived that would have allowed you to solve these problems faster, if only you knew how to derive them."

It was then that I realized the math we were doing in class was not the end game. I had believed that solving a rote problem was the intent, whereas, the intent was really to gain experience with the fundamentals in order to solve more complex problems — including problems that had not yet been solved. In the abstract this is a lesson that would serve me well later in life, long after I had abandoned pure mathematics for the challenge of innovating in financial services. In innovation, I find that many people want to know the formula — the process steps that they must follow to find the answer — when, in fact, very few of the problems we face have a textbook answer. The correct formula for innovation, if it exists at all, is rarely knowable at the outset. Knowing the fundamentals will unlock all of the wonderfully creative options you might have.

* * *

There is no correct answer to the question, "What does Today's Innovator look like?" Successful innovators come from all walks of life, with different educations, different experiences they draw upon to solve the most ambiguous and audacious business problems that exist. However, there are common threads — traits and skills that are found in many successful innovators. We will explore in *A Portrait of Today's Innovator* a series of *personas* that Today's Innovator might have to become.

It is not the intent for you to "check the box" on all of these personas. Not every persona will be relevant to every innovator, and for sure every challenge will require you to use a unique mix of these traits.

While all of the personas are comprised of traits that Today's Innovator might need to adopt, there is one persona that is a differentiator, one that sets the most competent innovators apart from the rest: Today's Innovator as an *Innovation Leader*. For that reason, we will explore in-depth what is required of an innovation leader, then finish with the remainder of the personas in an exploration of Today's Innovator as an *Individual*. Unlike the other parts of this book, you will not find a list of roadblocks related to Today's Innovator at the end, for in many respects, Today's Innovator is his or her own biggest limiter. As a master of the skills and traits found within *A Portrait of Today's Innovator,* you will meet no resistance, nor roadblocks, that cannot be overcome.

CHAPTER 22: TODAY'S INNOVATOR AS AN INNOVATION LEADER

I continued to develop my math skills in college, bouncing from periods of frustration, in which I had to memorize and practice fundamentals, to periods of productivity, where I was able to apply this foundation to solve complex problems. As a junior, I attended a math "retreat" with some of my classmates and professors. We were bussed out into the woods where we spent a weekend in a rustic lodge. Far removed from the sterile classrooms where we normally interacted, we were free to develop new norms and new ways of working together.

A Ford Motors executive showed up on day one of the retreat and introduced us to the problem we would be solving over the weekend: *The National Highway Safety Administration has some strict standards for the front and rear bumpers found on vehicles. They must be able to withstand a collision with a wall at a certain speed without causing any damage to any other part of the vehicle. Design the lowest cost bumper for Ford's new line of vehicles.*

We jumped right in, peppering the executive with questions about the new line of vehicles, about the test facility, about car bumper design, about the costs of materials and production, and much, much more.

Our approach to solving the problem was chaotic. There were no assigned leaders. No one had subject matter expertise (other than the executive, who generally left us alone, unless we had questions). We had to learn how to organize ourselves to answer the simplest of questions, such as, "What was the force of the collision?" More complex questions, such as, "What's the required strength of the reinforcement bar in the rear bumper?" seemed initially out of reach. Some working teams naturally formed. Some individuals worked independently. Some folks argued incessantly, while others made steady progress. There were many setbacks, and some spurts of genius.

At the end of each day we stopped to reflect on what was working well and what wasn't. By the third and final day, the chaos had subsided a bit and we had formed into three teams, each working on a part of the solution. Whether or not we designed an effective bumper that weekend, I'll never be sure, but we had developed into a set of high-performing teams that allowed us to take on the more complex questions that had initially seemed so out of reach.

After the final presentations, I recall one shy student saying to me, "Thank you for including me on your team." I didn't think much of it at the time, but there's a lesson to be learned from the seemingly insignificant exchange. I had not been given the title of "team leader." No one had. I hadn't viewed it as *my* team. I had just grown frustrated with the setbacks we were encountering in the beginning. Assuming this student had talent and expertise (otherwise, she wouldn't have been on the retreat), I had invited her into the conversation to help us — and she added a great deal of value. The lesson I learned was that developing high-performing teams doesn't happen on its own. It requires a designer, a *leader*, who creates environments where others feel empowered. With a simple gesture, this student went from (probably) feeling left out and apprehensive, to included and respected.

* * *

As Today's Innovator, you are the one who must upset the status quo when it stands in the way of progress, often displaying behaviors that seem back-channel, manipulative, counter-cultural, even rebellious. This is where it's so important to have aspirational values that are known and fully described so you can feel confident that even though you're cutting against the grain, you're *being* the change that you want to see. You may feel like Sisyphus, carrying the large rock of cultural change up a steep hill, only to be knocked back down every time you encounter someone whose job it is to keep the status quo in place.

At one of my previous employers, I broke the common convention of our siloed organization by phoning a technology systems expert from another department and inviting him to a marketing brainstorming meeting. He was eager to attend, but to attend he said he needed to charge his hour of time to a specific project. Turns out, I didn't have a formal project started, so I didn't know how to overcome this roadblock. I told him I'd get back to him, but I never did. We had the meeting without him. *The gravity of the status quo is strong.*

For the *innovation leader*, this pattern will repeat itself over and over, in perpetuity. When your goal is "continuous improvement of the organization towards higher levels of innovation maturity," you will *never* reach your destination. There will always be a few more steps to carry that rock up the hill. I've heard it said that innovation leaders in corporate environments only last, on average, about a year. I don't know whether that statistic is accurate, but I believe it. I can speak from experience that just three months of leading innovation in a Dysfunctional or Tentative Maturity organization is enough to drive most to give up.

The good thing is that it's not a lost cause. The organization can change, and the process of change, itself, can be rewarding. If the leader feels empowered, and if the leader creates an empowering environment for others, change can be like a tightly packed snowball at the top of a hill. It is slow progress at first, but as this chain of empowerment extends, the snowball picks up speed rolling down the hill and grows in size.

The term "leader" in *innovation leader* is not being used to describe someone who has the positional authority to direct others what to do, such as a *manager*. Leaders and managers are entirely different things.

As a manager, an innovator may direct the activities of another, and may evaluate their performance, but those activities are not sufficient enough to be called a leader. The innovation leader is someone who has made a choice to show empathy, to develop expertise, to be vulnerable, to experiment, and to live outside their comfort zone.

So, what is required of an innovation leader? Here, we explore six expectations of innovation leaders.

BUILDING HIGH-PERFORMING TEAMS

As Today's Innovator you must build and develop high-performing teams. Now, teams can take many forms. They can be dedicated to projects, or they can be comprised of volunteers. Teams can be cross-functional, mixing both internal and external resources. They can be temporary or permanent. Whatever the case, there are common features you'll find in these teams. The high-performing team is empathetic and honest with itself. It's creative and collaborative. It's fast when it can be, accurate when it needs to be. It's lean enough to be sufficiently agile. The team knows how to learn what's expected of it, and is courageously adaptable when it's not delivering. It's nimble when facing multiple obstacles, and resilient when it faces a mighty one. It anticipates the changes and pressures it may face, and can quickly respond when they present themselves. And high performing teams have both deep expertise and broad experience.

Teams don't start this way. These traits must be recruited for and developed. If the team is designed with self-reinforcing values, ultimately the team may not need to be managed closely, but it still needs to be *led* (of course, the leader doesn't need to be the same person every day). That is the role that you, as Today's Innovator, must play when no one else will, and it begins by regularly asking our Critical Question: *What does the organization require of my team in order to achieve its objectives?*

Simply by seeking answers to this question, you will reinforce many of the traits listed above: honest reflection, empathy, learning, creative problem solving, collaboration, and change readiness. By assessing and prioritizing the Critical Question's responses, the team gains knowledge, confidence, and courage. Finally, by acting on the highest-leverage opportunities (balancing effort/cost vs. risk/reward), the team becomes agile, nimble, responsive, resilient, and adaptive.

Again, any team can do this — it's not limited to the "innovation team" that's building the next $60 billion product.

SETTING CLEAR EXPECTATIONS

At one previous employer, I learned that our sales department was becoming openly critical of our innovation initiatives. When I inquired to learn more, it was a case of expectations not being clear or reinforced. They believed the innovation team's role was to build new products for them to sell, and were growing frustrated that they hadn't seen any new products launch. The simple answer to why they weren't seeing any new product launches is because *that wasn't what the innovation team was working on!* Conversely, the innovation team was relying upon feedback from the sales teams to gain new insight, but that feedback turned out to be hard to come by. The reason was simple: the sales team wasn't clear on what was expected of them, so they understandably prioritized their sales activity over their role in innovation.

Even if the vision, innovation strategy, objectives, and milestones have been communicated repeatedly, it cannot be assumed that everyone within the organization clearly understands theirs, their team's, or their department's role in innovation. Communication is just the starting point. As an innovation leader, you must ensure that these roles are well understood, or risk wasting energy by fighting hard against the status quo. This can be accomplished in several ways:

» By challenging individuals and teams to ask and answer the critical questions for themselves.

» By measuring the effectiveness of innovation strategy communications.

» By measuring the current state culture.

» By integrating and iterating the systems of innovation that have been agreed upon.

» By having regular conversations about what needs to be accomplished, and by when.

» By holding those accountable to delivering what is expected of them.

If a meeting structure or communication plan doesn't exist to reinforce communications, it needs to be built into the new innovation governance system. Once individuals and teams are clear on what's expected, they'll be more likely to grasp onto the new cultural trapeze, letting go of the old to begin to thrive in the new environment.

STRENGTHENING INNOVATION NETWORKS

As Today's Innovator you must build a strong, extensive *innovation network*, both within and outside of the organization. Your network must go beyond building personal relationships with the people within your network. It must design and define each individual's and team's role in innovation. Further, your network will be most effective when it is interconnected, not just a hub-and-spoke model with you at the center. For innovation, as a competency, to thrive, the researcher must be connected to the salesperson, the engineer must be connected to the attorney, the consultant must be connected to the operational expert, etc.

Different resources will undoubtedly thrive in different situations. The most effective innovation networks allow for each member to understand the abilities, constraints, expertise, level of influence, even the values and norms, of every other member. This allows them to leverage each other's strengths and balance their styles when innovating. It doesn't mean each member needs to know everything about every other member, but rather, it means that this information is *knowable* and *accessible*. It may be sufficient that you establish common language and frameworks, which self-reinforce that teams leverage strengths and balance styles.

The design of a network should consider what skills and thinking styles are required for the type of innovation that the organization must deliver. Robust innovation networks include researchers, analysts, designers, facilitators, executives, developers, wire-framers, customers, complementary thinkers, know-it-alls, soothsayers, musicians, mothers, etc. What's important is that the network is designed so that it doesn't think the same way as the folks accountable for delivering the innovation objectives. It should be comprised of those who will challenge the assumptions and take the work in a new direction.

The process of building and expanding a network is likely to uncover opportunities for rapid experimentation that might have otherwise been hidden. Innovation leaders will be among the first to see possibilities, such as taking an existing organizational competency and testing it in a new market. As an innovation leader, it is your role to make the network connections and provide the environment and resources for these experiments to happen. Further, it is your role to teach others, by example, that it is safe and rewarding to influence this type of innovation.

LEADING CHANGE EMPATHETICALLY

With all this talk of fast-paced execution, experimentation, innovation portfolios, etc. it is fair to see that you will experience and create a considerable amount of change. In a fast-paced environment, it can be difficult for all of those who are busy executing to take the time to appreciate and understand the context for all the changes that are occurring around them.

As Today's Innovator, you must take care to measure and manage the morale of those who are subject to all of the changes that innovation programs cause. The pressure to be fast-paced and change-oriented must be balanced with an empathy for those who are affected. Within a fast-paced environment, employees can feel overwhelmed by the sheer number of projects they are involved in. They can lose track of commitments that they've made. They can experience stress caused by knowing they are expected to deliver something that they simply don't have the bandwidth to deliver.

While such an environment is not ideal, there are some mitigating approaches to consider. One such approach is to maintain a *backlog* of all ideas, features, technologies, projects, etc. that could be considered, but that aren't currently in-flight. Another might be to attach a ritual to the completion of work, so that lingering or outstanding tasks that might be associated with work that others consider complete don't contribute to stress.

BEING ACCOUNTABLE

If you display all the traits listed above, you will become a highly visible employee within an expanded network who is earning higher levels of responsibility. With this visibility comes an accountability to walk the talk of the organization's innovation competency. This begins with accountability to yourself to maintain engagement and perspective, to seek and become responsive to feedback, and to trust and coach others rather than to criticize. It extends to your accountability to the team and organization to hold others accountable to the new standards. This requires the discipline to not discriminate, to tactfully call out counter-cultural behaviors, to recognize when the team is reverting to old norms or behaviors, and to celebrate progress when it is made.

As an innovation leader, you must be as committed to spending time working on your team as you are working within your team, ensuring that all are orienting well to new objectives, values, and systems.

BUILDING EMPOWERED EMPLOYEES

Creating the environment where innovation can thrive inside of an organization cannot be accomplished alone. It requires many people of various backgrounds to measure, design, plan, and execute the rewiring. The change process is complex and non-linear and cannot be mapped end-to-end with any reasonable degree of certainty. Fortunately, as progress is made towards a future state in which the innovation competency is well developed, steadily improving, and self-sustaining, employees will begin to feel more comfortable and more confident in the new environment. As much as the executives and designers will want to control the change, the aspirational vision and values will become ingrained into the essence of the rewired organizations, allowing the reins to be loosened. Employees will learn to act as the change agents by their own accord. They'll create communities with common interests that will initiate new changes. The task of the initial team that sets the change in motion ultimately becomes to measure and course correct, as needed. This newly-formed, clear, confident, safe, competent, and motivated state of mind that employees will feel is *empowerment.*

Empowerment is not something you can give to someone; it's not something a manager can give to an employee. Empowerment is a feeling someone must have, a feeling built up and reinforced by the environment that it lives in. As an innovation leader, you must learn how to build these environments — where employees feel safe taking risks, where they explore on their own, where they're curious, where they are experts, and where they, themselves, can lead. The difference between a leader and a manager is that the latter directs resources, whereas, the leader creates the environment where others feel empowered to direct themselves, and where others can lead.

* * *

When I first earned the title of Chief Innovation Officer, employees who desired change and didn't know how to create it on their own would email me their improvement ideas. Many employees had no outlet for their ideas, or even feared sharing their ideas. The best they could hope for is that someone else would take and execute *their* idea. This was decidedly not an empowering environment.

For the first year or so, I collected these ideas, hoping to find a landing place for them. They were all over the place — suggesting everything from a new marketing angle, to a new vacuuming schedule for the office. I would reassure the employee who submitted the idea that we valued it and that I would pass it along to the proper team to consider. The success rate on those ideas was 0%. And employees were wondering what was happening to them. The monkey was on my back.

A funny thing happened about a year into our innovation program. As the innovation strategy and culture became better defined, the nature of the ideas that came into my inbox began to change. Some were now specific to a business problem that had been articulated, some were asking me for help in finding the best place to take their idea, and some were seeking my permission to put an idea into action. There was new context and a new confidence growing that was making the ideas more relevant and more achievable. This was a notable change, to be sure, but it wasn't the desired end state.

Another year into the program I was able to detect yet another shift had occurred. I was receiving fewer and fewer *ideas* flowing into my inbox. They were being replaced with success stories of how employees had recognized something that needed to be addressed and had figured out how to address it themselves. Employees had stopped asking for permission and were ready to ask for forgiveness! To the occasional idea that trickled in, I would simply reply, "No one will love your idea more than you," sending them back to influence the execution of the idea on their own. The empowering environment that we had built was beginning to produce the intended result, a *culture of innovation* in which each employee knew enough and felt supported enough to innovate on their own. Each employee had become an *innovator*.

CHAPTER 23: TODAY'S INNOVATOR AS AN INDIVIDUAL

At this point, we've addressed critical questions #1 and #2, related to designing the environment that the organization needs, and related to becoming an innovation leader who adapts teams to what the organization needs, respectively. We haven't explicitly examined critical question #3: *Who does the organization need me to be?*

In those eight words you can find the recipe for being a great innovator. As Today's Innovator, you must first understand the needs of the organization, then must adapt to become what, or who, it needs you to be. In this final chapter, we'll explore seven additional *personas* that you, as Today's Innovator, might adopt as an *individual*. Again, it is not the intent for you to "check the box" on all of these personas. Instead, become familiar with them, and keep them in mind as you determine who the organization needs you to be.

So, just who does Today's Innovator need to be?

THE OBSERVER

As the *observer*, you must be aware, constantly listening, questioning, and learning. *Empathy* is the critical skill required: empathy to appreciate what's working well, and what's not; empathy to recognize what stressors the team and its resources are facing; and empathy to uncover and understand the needs and pain points of customers. It's easy to fall into the trap that, as an innovator, it is you who must have the answers. But it is the genius who asks the best questions! Fall in love with the problems you face. Surround yourself with people who know more than you, who you can learn from, who can show you what to do.

THE EXPERT

Of course, the observer role will not always be what's required. As the *expert*, you seek insight to become better, faster, and more knowledgeable. The expertise you develop and practice will give you confidence to push against forces, to improve features, and help others succeed. Toggling between the observer role and the expert role is the process of developing insight, then developing solutions. Create a plan to develop expertise in the disciplines that will differentiate your innovation program from others. Others will come to rely on you and value you for your expertise. Whether it's in machine learning, customer experience design, emerging technologies, finance, or design thinking, your expertise will become your comfort zone.

THE TEAMMATE

As the *teammate*, your role is to support others, offer them guidance, and make offers to take on the tasks required to achieve the team's objectives. The teammate lifts others up by empathizing, meeting the team where they are, then sharing knowledge and expertise to allow others to perform at their highest level. Being a great teammate doesn't always require interpersonal connections; it can be as simple as developing resources such as innovation toolkits for others to reference, or taking a training course on a subject that will benefit the team as a whole.

THE BUILDER

Probably the most common persona associated with innovators is the *builder*. As the builder, you are a visionary, a creative genius, who connects people and ideas to improve conditions and solve problems. The builder infuses new technologies, new partnerships, and new sciences into old ideas. Like Emmet in the popular *Lego Movie,* as the builder you should thrive when there are no instructions. In innovation, the blueprints for success are rarely known. You should learn to excel in situations where outcomes are not well-defined, where they're intangible and ambiguous. As the builder, don't complain about *what is* and *what isn't,* instead ask "What would it look like if...?" or "How could we...?"

THE AGITATOR

Creativity doesn't occur when everyone is comfortable. As the *agitator,* you create angst, ignore convention, and upset the status quo to inspire new thinking. Organizations that are complacent or stuck in the status quo will not have the perspective or desire required to create truly innovative solutions. As Today's Innovator, you must channel your frustration over the organization's inability to keep pace with the explosion of digital, social, technological, and global change into new thinking. Creativity arises when you make the choice not to continue to play by the rules (written and unwritten) which have led you to where you are today. As the agitator, forget which sandbox you are supposed to be playing in, then challenge others to do the same.

THE SALESMAN

As the *salesman,* you must motivate others to prepare for change, to change themselves, and to innovate. You must learn how to negotiate power structures and political currents in the organization to influence decisions — both in cases where the rules are well-known, such as in creating and pitching a business case that aligns with predefined screening criteria in order to fund innovation, and where they are unknown, such as in developing strong relationships that may be of benefit later. As a salesman, you are an actor, performing every day, managing perceptions of yourself and of innovation.

THE INITIATOR

As Today's Innovator, it is not enough for you to simply adapt to change, as a chameleon who blends in with his environment. You must be the *initiator*: an agent of change who blazes new trails, who relentlessly pursues strategic vectors, and who finds and enlists employees as allies in change. This requires the ability to make swift decisions in the absence of data, or in the absence of direction. You must understand how your experiences and assumptions might bias such decisions, and work to expand your own, and your organization's worldview. Asking and answering the Critical Questions every day, as the initiator you make the choice to do the right thing for the organization, for the team, and for customers, even if it cuts against the grain.

* * *

It is no longer sufficient to rely on deep subject matter expertise to become an effective innovator. Today's Innovator must be rooted in that expertise, but must be able to look up from what's in the immediate vicinity to understand how the world is changing. You'll be expected to create high-functioning networks and high-performing teams, communicate effectively, and influence decisions outside of your own domain of expertise. This type of leadership — *innovation leadership* — does not come naturally. It requires dedication, attention, coaching, experience, and risk taking. And, it will ruffle feathers from time-to-time. You must balance this agitation with a keen business and political acumen that comes from being curious and empathetic towards the organization and its circumstances.

CHAPTER 24: INNOVATION MATURITY STAGES: TODAY'S INNOVATOR

During my career, I've experienced several periods of stagnation in my development as an innovator. But, it has always been the case that a period of tremendous growth would follow, usually coming at times when I felt the most inadequate, most underprepared, and most challenged to perform at a high level.

Perhaps that's to be expected as an innovator who is required to thrive in uncertainty, required to drive change, required to upset the status quo. Higher levels of performance will require higher levels of maturity. Let's revisit the Maturity Stages to further illustrate how you, as Today's Innovator, may change through the various stages.

DYSFUNCTIONAL MATURITY STAGE

Today's Innovator in a Dysfunctional Maturity organization is excited, curious, and innocently unaware of the challenges to come. The organization is unsure of what will come from innovation. You have many more questions than answers, and more aspirations than accomplishments.

TENTATIVE MATURITY STAGE

Today's Innovator in a Tentative Maturity organization is stretched, making strides, yet unable to determine why it's so challenging to gain traction. The organization is committing to an innovation strategy, and is learning that it will have to work differently. You know what's not working, and you are working hard to overcome resistance and roadblocks.

CONFIDENT MATURITY STAGE

Today's Innovator in a Confident Maturity organization is humbled, hardened, and frustrated that the organization can't seem to get out of its own way. Parts of the organization are beginning to feel empowered to execute the innovation strategy. You have built strong networks, talented teams, and are holding everyone accountable to what they've committed to.

COMPETENT MASTERY STAGE

Today's Innovator in a Competent Mastery organization is an explorer, a leader, and a change agent. The organization is pursuing innovative strategic vectors and has built the environment to succeed. You possess deep expertise, broad influence, and you work to stay ahead of the challenges to come.

CHAPTER 25: GO, INNOVATE!

I only slept a couple of hours the night before my Master's thesis defense. I had decided I would wake up at 4:00 AM to arrive on campus, well before anyone else, allowing me one last early-morning study session. This earned me the closest parking spot I'd ever had to the math building.

Sitting in my car, I felt nervous, unsure of what types of questions I would be asked. The sun was just coming up. Looking around, I saw the campus was peaceful; there wasn't a soul in sight. Taking a deep breath, I pushed open my car door until it bumped into something soft.

"Oh, I'm sorry," said a voice from outside my car, startling me.

"Who's there?" I asked, surprised, as I hadn't seen anyone around.

His face peeked out from behind my open car door, then he stepped into full view.

Before me stood a man, no more than three feet tall. He looked me in the eye and spoke, "I didn't expect your door to open."

"Did I hit you?" I replied, still trying to orient myself to what was happening.

"Yes, but it's okay. I'm fine," he said with a laugh, smiling from ear-to-ear.

His smile put me at ease. My mind had been on my math. Hitting a little person with my car door had caught me quite a bit off-guard. I'm sure I was staring at his stature as I struggled to find my next words.

"Well, it's me who should be sorry!" I finally exclaimed.

"It's *okay*," he reassured me, still smiling.

He backed up as I grabbed my bag and exited the car.

"You're here early," he said to me, starting conversation.

I explained that I normally wouldn't arrive this early, but was hoping to get a few hours of studying in before my Master's thesis defense. As I spoke, I noticed we had started walking down the sidewalk together towards the main campus.

"Well, are you prepared?" he asked.

"I've been studying for weeks, but I'm not feeling great. There are a lot of things they could ask me that I'm not confident about."

"Where are you from?" he asked, changing the subject.

We chatted back-and-forth as we walked the quarter mile to the math building, covering all the standard topics — where home was, the weather, sports, etc. We tied up the loose ends of the conversation standing in front of the door to the building.

"You're going to do great," he proclaimed, changing the subject back to my thesis defense.

"How do you know?"

"I just know," he said confidently. "You got this."

I think he may have winked at me as he turned and walked away. I had never seen him before, and I would never see him again.

As I later stepped into the classroom where I would earn my Master's degree, I remembered my exchange with the little man I'd hit with my car door and I laughed aloud. Relaxed, I successfully defended my position, recalling his simple words, "You got this," with each challenging question I fielded.

My new friend from that morning had done just enough to eliminate any doubt I'd had about my readiness. His kind words and good cheer had lifted me up. If I'd felt *doubt* as I defended my position, it could have been debilitating, eating me up and leading me to second-guess my instincts. Instead, I'd felt only *uncertainty* about what questions would be asked.

The questions they would ask me could not be known in advance. But, I had improved my odds of success by anticipating the types of questions that might be asked and honing my general math skills.

It was during my defense that I learned I thrive in uncertain, unpredictable circumstances. I felt empowered then, and have tried to recreate this feeling many times since, replacing any doubt that I feel with a confident reminder that I am as prepared as I could be.

With the level of uncertainty that exists in the world today, it could be easy to become paralyzed, not knowing which threats to ward off and which opportunities to pursue. One strategy is hiding from changes that are to come, to doubt your ability to affect change, trying instead to preserve the status quo for as long as possible. But isn't it better to both preserve the best parts of the status quo *and* get yourself in the best position to deal with what changes will come?

This is your job as Today's Innovator, to become competent enough to be able to thrive in an aggressively changing world, all while working within an organizational system that has a certain set of constraints. By developing an innovative organizational mindset, one that understands how to plan for change and has a culture that responds appropriately, you can feel empowered. Once that mindset is in place, there is only one thing left for you to do… *Go, innovate!*

ABOUT AARON PROIETTI

Aaron Proietti is an innovation expert with seventeen years of experience innovating in complex organizations. Most recently, at Transamerica, a multinational, Fortune 500 insurance company, Aaron built and led the company's Insights & Innovation department, consisting of six centers of excellence designed to fuel innovation. As Chief Innovation Officer, he led a division-wide effort to transform the culture of 6,000 employees to a culture of innovation, collaboration, and trust. As Chief Customer Advocate, he merged the company's customer-centric service strategy with its forward-looking innovation strategy. And, as the Head of Marketing Innovation, he built and staffed a cutting-edge Research & Development team tasked with building customer experiences of the future and integrating them back into Transamerica's core business.

After getting his Master's Degree in Applied Mathematics from Georgia Tech, Aaron got his career started as a Data Analyst at Capital One, one of the nation's largest banks — a role that for sure would be called a Data Scientist today. It is there that he gained his first exposure to innovation as part of a team that developed new products and processes that contributed over $50 million per year. Aaron later worked as a Product Owner in Capital One's "Invention Factory," as well as several other roles that would shape his career as an innovator. It is at Capital One where Aaron learned the value a strong corporate culture has in driving innovation. He left Capital One in 2007 to gain experience in the startup environment, working to develop a new way of packaging and selling life insurance.

In 2016, at the age of forty, Aaron stepped away from the corporate grind to decompress and reevaluate his career trajectory. He founded Adaptivity Enterprises, LLC, and todaysinnovator.com to "help the world thrive amidst accelerating pace of change" by writing, speaking at conferences, coaching innovation leaders, and helping organizations design and build their innovation competency. Aaron has been a regular writing contributor at InnovationLeader.com and Insurance Thought Leadership.